1ST AIR COMMANDO GROUP

Any Place, Any Time, Anywhere

Major R. D. Van Wagner

Military History Series 86-1

1986

Air Command and Staff College
Maxwell Air Force Base
Montgomery, Alabama 36112

THE MILITARY HISTORY SERIES:

The United States Air Force Air Command and Staff College, in cooperation with the ACSC Foundation, publishes the Military History Series. The purpose of the series is to help professional military officers to gain a greater appreciation for the lessons which may be derived from the military past.

Disclaimer:

Distribution Statement:

TABLE OF CONTENTS

LIST OF ILLUSTRATIONS

TABLES

FIGURES

FOREWORD

I am pleased to introduce this study, the third in the Air Command and Staff College's Military History Series, for your reading enjoyment and reflection. The study of history can be very instructive and, while history never repeats itself exactly, there are parallel themes and approaches that can provide us with fresh perspectives and creative insights.

Low-intensity conflict is a contemporary concern and many analysts believe that this is the type of challenge increasingly likely to confront the United States. Unfortunately, many observers also believe that the United States is least prepared to participate successfully at this level of conflict. This monograph provides the opportunity to acquire fresh perspectives from the study of Air Commando operations in the China-Burma-India theater during the Second World War. As such, this work provides contemporary military officers and defense planners with valuable lessons concerning low-intensity conflict. Finally, this monograph is well written, entertaining, and will contribute to that professional knowledge base we all need in order to successfully confront the challenges to U.S. national security throughout the remainder of the twentieth century and beyond.

Frank E. Willis
Brigadier General, USAF
Commandant

PREFACE

The only thing harder than getting a new idea into the military mind is to get an old one out.

B. H. Liddell Hart (9:190)

This work examines the 1st Air Commando Group of World War II—an experiment looking toward future air warfare. Employed in the China-Burma-India Theater, the organization made military history by conducting the first Allied all-aerial invasion—Operation THURSDAY. Because of more glamorous campaigns in Europe and the Pacific, THURSDAY and the 1st Air Commandos have been generally overlooked by military historians. This study calls attention to that lost piece of airpower history; however, it is not a definitive work. That undertaking would be enormous considering the group never published a unit history, instead adopting the theme: "To hell with the paper work, go out and fight." Therefore, this account focuses on the circumstances which brought about the requirement for and the employment of the 1st Air Commando Group in Burma during the Spring of 1944. By using an unorthodox strategy, the group serves as a model organization for use in unconventional conflicts today.

The primary impetus for this study of the 1st Air Commando Group is my father, Fred H. Van Wagner. He joined the air commandos after their deployment to India but before Operation THURSDAY. Greatly influenced by the events and camaraderie experienced in India, he passed on his acquired values and philosophy to me. This study has been well worth the time spent; it has helped me to know my father better. Therefore, with warmth and love, I dedicate my research project to him.

xi

This study would not have been possible without the help of many former members of the 1st Air Commando Group. I am grateful to Gen John R. Alison, co-commander of the unit, for his contribution and participation. I hold a great respect for him and the accomplishments of his organization. I was also aided by the men of the 1st Air Commando Association. Particularly, I wish to express my appreciation to the association secretary, Robert Moist, for his time and information. Additionally, interviews with Arthur Burrel; Frank Clifford; Joseph Cochran; Lemuel Davis; John Derdak; Thomas Doherty; Patrick Driscoll; Dr. Cortez Enloe; Paul Forcey; Allen Hall, Jr.; Neville Hogan; John Hyland; Felix Lockman, Jr.; Joseph Lysowski; Stamford Robertson; Raymond Ruksas; Lloyd Samp; Howard Smith; Tom Taketa; Vincent Ulery; and F. H. Van Wagner provided invaluable insights. Their responses to my questions and enthusiastic support of this endeavor were an inspiration.

Equally important to my work was the assistance of organizations and people at Maxwell AFB. I am indebted to the personnel of the USAF Historical Research Center, Herb Huie of the Graphic Arts organization, and to the Photographic Shop. I would like to formally thank my advisor, Lt Col Robert Gregory, for his encouragement, technical assistance, and advice. Finally, I would be remiss if I did not also thank the members of my family for their patience and understanding during this task. Many kind people have helped and encouraged me in writing this account; I thank them all.

Introduction

THE 1ST AIR COMMANDO GROUP

Broadway

It's just a field covered with buffalo grass, in the midst of a jungle where it has slept for countless years under the Burmese sun. Marked on no map, it was unknown and nameless until the necessities of war gave it sudden importance.

Then one night many men in gliders slipped like mammoth eagles down through the hazy moonlight, making history in aerial warfare and giving to it the name of "Broadway Burma."

For many of these men this spot was the end of the road; but now there is little to suggest the madness of that first night or the horror of succeeding nights and days.

A mass of twisted metal, rusting and half covered by the jungle growth . . . and a deep hole, now partly healed with buffalo grass, marks accurately the spot where many died.

It's sacred now, this once worthless ground like many other "Broadways" with other names. But the buffalo grass will grow, and the jungle will creep in and cover the carved panel, and the wooden cross will rot. And slowly, it will be again worthless ground—unless we remember.

— Paul L. Bissell
Lt Col, USAAF (33:9–10)

The story of Broadway and Operation THURSDAY, the event reverently described above, is one of imagination, courage, and tragedy. This all-aerial invasion took place in the "ignored" China-Burma-India Theater on the other side of the world. Overshadowed by the events in Europe and the Pacific, Operation THURSDAY is now largely forgotten by all except the units that participated. This is the story of one of those units.

The 1st Air Commando Group was sired by General of the Army Henry H. Arnold and brought to life by the imagination of two men, Lt Col Philip G. Cochran and Lt Col John R. Alison. In gathering men of character and tenacity, these two visionaries molded a unit which had to overcome orthodox military minds, paralyzing fear, and Burma's impregnable terrain before taking the fight to the Japanese.

With a focus on the might and flexibility of air power, Cochran and Alison constructed an experimental unit which cut across the structured lines of conventional organizations. Forming an air arsenal which was totally unique in its composition and application, they combined the firepower of fighters and bombers with the logistical tentacles of transports, gliders, and light planes to reach far behind Japanese lines.

By landing soldiers beyond those line, the Allies for the first time, used airpower for the backbone of an invasion. On a moonlit night in March 1944, the 1st Air Commandos flew more than 200 miles behind the Japanese defenses on the Indo-Burmese border to establish an airfield named Broadway in the midst of enemy-held territory. From this "beachhead" the Allies poured more than 9,000 specially trained soldiers onto the back porch of Japan's extended empire. The actions of the 1st Air Commandos breathed life into the stagnant China-Burma-India Theater and turned defeatism into victory.

The story of the 1st Air Commando Group has its origins deeply rooted in the Japanese march across Southeast Asia. The terror and chaos that emanated from the wake of the Nippon advance established the circumstances and the need for the formation of the 1st Air Commando Group. In answer to Lt Col Bissell's entreaty, this work examines the backdrop of Burma, traces the lineage of the commandos, and recalls the events of Operation THURSDAY so that Broadway will never again become "worthless ground."

Chapter One

BURMA: THE PROBLEM

Bolstered by their recent successful attack on Pearl Harbor, Japanese strategists announced their intention to invade the small country of Burma on 23 December 1941. On that date, the Japanese launched an air raid on the key Burmese port of Rangoon. The damage inflicted by the raid was questionable; the intent of the Japanese action, however, was well defined and of tremendous strategic impact. From the secure, sophisticated shores of the United States, this attack was not well publicized and consequently, scarcely understood. Why would the Nippon Empire be interested in the obscure land of Burma? For those aware of that sleepy nation in Southeast Asia, the question posed was about the Burmese defensive capability. What resistance would the Japanese soldiers face as they tried to take such a rugged and foreboding land? And finally, would this British colony hold out against the might of the Emperor's finest troops? How these questions were answered during the invasion of Burma would affect future campaign strategy.

The question of "why?" is answered by an analysis of the Japanese desire to use Burma as a wedge, a springboard, and a shield (44:4). By appealing to all of these desires, Burma promised to be a vitally strategic trophy.

In accordance with the 1927 Tanaka Memorial, Japan had annexed Manchuria in 1931, and in 1937, had begun a systematic march on China's major cities of Peking, Tientsin, Shanghai, Nanking, and Hankow. When finished, most of China was effectively cut off from the outer world. By 1941, the Japanese had fundamentally closed the door on China, but resistance was soon being met with the help of a supply line, the Burma Road, that

1

extended from India through Burma to the small mountain town of Kunming in the Yunnan province of China.

As they looked at Burma, the Japanese strategists saw a wedge—a way to stop China's flow of munitions, equipment, and provisions (43:1673). The deep mountains provided a natural barrier to conclusively seal off China and starve her into submission. With Burma occupied, the Japanese could stabilize China and release the Nippon continental forces for other potential conquests (44:4).

The Chinese element may have been the impetus for the invasion, but Japan saw other strategic prizes in Burma. As well as establishing a roadblock for Chinese supplies, Burma also could become the springboard for an offensive into the riches of India. The Japanese sensed an opportunity to take advantage of civil unrest, stirred by India's Mohandas K. Gandhi, to absorb the greatest British colony in Asia (27:258–259). If Japan invaded, they anticipated the support of the Indian population to chase the British out of India.

India was indeed a prize worth having, as great, if not more so, than China itself. World War I had given a stimulus to commercialization in India; in 1941 she offered an economy with burgeoning industrial capability. Production of coal and cotton had begun before 1920, but since that time, the iron and steel, arms and munition, and chemical industries had emerged with gusto (15:52–59).

Most important though was the Japanese grand strategy to overrun India and link up with a planned German push in Persia under the command of German General Erwin Rommel (44:4). Burma was the way to people, industry, and a possible strategic union; indeed the very idea of Burma brought a gleam of covetousness to the eyes of the Japanese generals.

As a pivot point, Burma offered China and India, but Burma, by itself, also beckoned to the Japanese. Three reasons are given—rice, natural resources, and natural defense. In 1940, the mainstay of Burma's internal and external economy was rice, almost 12,000,000 acres were under cultivation. To Japan, Burma represented a "rice bowl" capable of producing nearly 8,000,000 tons of this staple crop. Japan felt Burma's export of 3,000,000 tons of rice could be rechannelled to its already overextended Imperial Army (6:185–186). Additionally, Burma of-

2

Figure 1. The Burma Road.

fered an abundance of natural resources, primarily oil and manganese. Finally, a Japanese-occupied Burma would act as a barrier or shield for the entire Far East territory (44:4). Japanese occupation of Burma would put much distance between the Allies and Japan's new possessions of the Philippines, French Indochina, Thailand, Singapore, and the Dutch East Indies.

For the question of "why?" there was plenty of rationale. With so many reasons to invade—China, India, and Burma's food and natural resources, the question of the unknown Burmese defense plans waited to be answered. The only way to find out was to try, and that the Japanese decided to do in earnest when the new year, 1942, rolled around.

There were three factors which comprised the British defensive scheme. Collectively the Japanese had to overcome them all. They were as follows:

(1) The impact of Burma's rugged geography,
(2) The effect of the Burmese climatic conditions, and
(3) The preparedness of Burma's defense (44:2–3).

Separately they posed no appreciable problem, but together, each contributed to a viable British plan for the defense of Burma against the Japanese invasion.

Geographically speaking, Burma resembled a waterfall. All the natural elements which composed Burma paralleled each other running from north to south—the mountains, the rivers, the roads, her central plain, her valleys and even the railway. Consequently travel in Burma from east to west was an enterprise contrary to the rules of nature. Burma's sudden and irregular mountains isolated one valley from another. The roads connecting these valleys snaked across the mountains and progress was always slow (14:141). Additionally, the mountainsides were covered with jungles thick enough to form a natural canopy. Hiding beneath this umbrella were leeches, malaria-carrying mosquitoes, and diseases by the score.

It was, therefore, obvious for the British to assume that an invader would be confined to the meager road system, railroads, or the great rivers. If given a choice, travellers generally used the waterways because Burma possessed two major and three smaller river systems. The largest river, the Irrawaddy, flowed swiftly

Figure 2. Southeast Asia, Circa 1942.

5

down the center of the country and was joined from the northwest by the next largest in size, the Chindwin. Together these two mammoth rivers provided over 15,000 miles of navigable waters to the near geographic center of Burma (45:28).

Because of the north/south topography of Burma, choke points—the confluence of rivers, roads and railroads—were commonplace. Herein was the defensive strength of Burma. Under the circumstances, the British felt sure the Japanese could be held at bay by a relatively small force taking advantage of the natural contours and configuration of the land.

The British also felt time was on their side in Burma because of the recurring monsoons. Rain! Probably the most dominant feature of Burma was the monsoons. Lasting from mid-May until late October, the monsoons limited all military operations to the dry season. Rainfalls varied from about 200 inches in the area of Rangoon, 100 inches in the Irrawaddy Delta, 80 inches in the hills, and up to 45 inches in the dry zone of North Central Burma (45:5). The effect of the rain was not only the ankle deep mud and mire, but also the enervating monotony of the incessant downpour. The British hoped topography would slow down the Japanese enough so the monsoons could deliver the knockout punch. Key to British success was their ability to hold out until mid-May; this key was in the hand of General Archibald Wavell, Commander-in-Chief of British Forces, India.

When the military responsibility for Burma was transferred from Singapore to India on 12 December 1941, Gen Wavell was greatly concerned by the extent of unpreparedness in Burma's defense. He did concede, however, it was understandable because Burma was protected from sea invasion by Singapore and from land attack by three friendly neighbors. As long as Singapore, Thailand, Indochina, and India remained strong, there was no need for a buildup in Burma (43:1667–1668).

This dependence on regional stability was reinforced by the fact the Burmese Army had only been activated since April 1937. By late 1941, Burma had two British infantry battalions, two Indian infantry brigades, eight battalions of Burma Rifles, four mountain artillery batteries, and the equivalent of six battalions of the Burma Frontier Force. The latter mostly worked under the control of the Civil Power and had little fighting value (43:1667–1669). The forces available for the defense of Burma

6

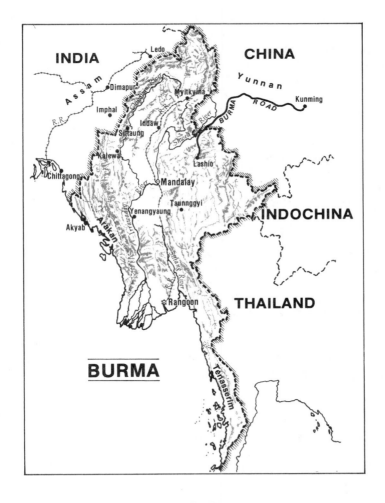

Figure 3. Burma.

7

were only partially trained and almost without artillery, signal equipment, and anti-aircraft weapons (7:Map 127). The air force was practically non-existent. It consisted of one fighter squadron equipped with Brewster Buffaloes (43:1668).

To assist in the defense of Burma, an offer by China's Generalissimo Chiang Kai-shek, complicated by the Chinese demand for separate lines of communication, was finally accepted by Gen Wavell. It must be stated, however, that "Britain . . . had little respect for China's military capacity." (26:235)

Lacking equipment, aircraft, manpower, and training, the military was clearly the weak link in the Burma defense plan. Gen Wavell counted on India for possible reinforcements and was beginning to mobilize for Burma's defense when Japan dropped its first bombs on Rangoon (43:1668–1671).

For Gen Wavell and India Command the combination of two factors, terrain and national defense, was hoped to be sufficient to impede the Japanese until arrival of the monsoons. Gen Wavell felt that when the operation resumed again in late October, he would have a sufficiently strong army in place to resist the Japanese. In matter of fact, Gen Wavell's hope proved to be groundless. His forces could not even hold out until mid-May.

In systematic fashion, the Japanese Army attacked first the weakest link in the military infrastructure of Burma, established air superiority, and then raced against the monsoons to overtake the British and Chinese Armies (43:1670–1675). The complete story of the Battle of Burma cannot possibly be undertaken here, but a brief synopsis of the events will establish the situation and provide a frame of reference.

Before ever dropping a bomb or setting foot on Burma soil, the Japanese plan for the Southeast Asia region foreshadowed the demise of the British in Burma. The first step in their plan, the occupation of Thailand, was accomplished after only eight hours of fighting. By December 1941, they converged their resources on the Malay Peninsula and the British fortress of Singapore. The Emperor's master plan called for the fall of the British citadel in 100 days. Unfortunately for the British, on 15 February 1942, the Japanese took Singapore 70 days after initiating action (1:114–116).

With the defeat of Singapore, Burma's protection from a sea invasion was lost; the swiftness of the Japanese occupation of the vital links of Thailand and Singapore now left Burma naked. Gen Wavell could not react quickly enough to overcome the Nippon momentum. Additional troops from the 16th Indian Brigade were still landing at Rangoon when the Japanese 15th Army, under Lt Gen Shojira Iida, began its move on Burma in strength (43:1667-1669).

Initially securing airfields along the Tenasserim coast, Gen Iida then mounted his attack on the port of Rangoon itself. All hope for Rangoon was doomed when a British commander ordered the Sittang Bridge destroyed, leaving hundreds of British troops stranded on the Japanese side (26:253-254). With just a remnant of an army, the British were unable to withstand the Japanese assaults on Rangoon. On 8 March, British General the Right Honourable Sir Harold Alexander abandoned the port city and set in motion the longest and most inglorious retreat in British military history (22:15-30). During this "strategic withdrawal" two personalities emerged, British MGen William J. Slim and American Lt Gen Joseph W. Stilwell. From a tactical perspective, their viewpoint of the rout showed the chaos and terror of the tumultous flight back to India.

Gen Slim had spent most of his career in the Indian Army; during the 1942 campaign he commanded the Burma Corps, consisting of the 17th Indian Division and the 1st Burma Division. When the Japanese invaded, the British were unprepared for the speed of the Japanese advance. While the British troops were roadbound and expected the Japanese to be likewise, the truth was the opposite. The Japanese were able to use the jungle to their advantage. They often divided into small units and by-passed enemy troop movements. Well behind the British lines, they would establish roadblocks by felling trees and emplacing machine guns (26:245;27:60). Gen Slim's command was particularly vulnerable to this type of attack as they had been trained for mechanized desert warfare (21:8).

Using this method, the Japanese continued to harass Gen Slim by pushing the Burma Corps northward along the Irrawaddy Valley toward the oil fields of Yenangyaung. Forced to live on bully beef and biscuits, Slim's troops were strafed by Japanese planes, suffered from lack of water, and became enveloped by Japanese troops. Under these conditions, he gave the order to blow up the oil fields before they fell into the hands of the advancing horde (21:49–59).

With no more reasons to stay and fight in Burma, Slim began a general retreat. At the Chindwin River, Slim ordered his men to cross at the only available point, the Basin—a natural site for ambush. With Gurkhas, fierce soldiers from Nepal, to guard the rear of his columns, Slim began the crossing only to learn the Gurkhas' radio had failed and Japanese troops were overrunning the crossing area. Gen Slim continued to direct the decaying situation until all his men boarded the last ferry and made it to safety on the other side (21:78–84).

Fortunately, the Japanese decided not to press the attack and Gen Slim finally marched into India on 16 May. With him were over 12,000 troops; more importantly, he left almost 13,000 troops behind (8:84).

For Gen Stilwell, the results were the same and the performance of the Chinese reinforced British perceptions. Arriving in Chungking just two days before the fall of Rangoon, Stilwell was immediately placed in command of all the Chinese troops in Burma. His job was to hold the Sittang Valley and the railroad between Rangoon and Mandalay. To protect Northern Burma, Gen Alexander planned to establish a defensive line about 150 miles north of Rangoon. Seeing the disadvantages of this strategy, Gen Stilwell proposed a counter-offensive using the Chinese 5th Army's 22nd and 96th Divisions. However, Gen Chiang Kai-shek delayed approval; then MGen Tu Yu-ming found excuses and finally utterly refused to fight, fearing the 96th Division might lose the only field artillery in the Chinese Army (36:272–289).

Other instances were noted of the Chinese lack of resolve. Attacked by a Japanese regiment, Stilwell lost the Chinese 55th Division when they fled from an inferior Japanese force and vanished. His one bright spot, the retaking of Taunnggyi, was accomplished only after offering the Chinese troops monetary rewards. But that too came to nought as the Japanese detoured around the town and drove on to Lashio and the Burma Road (26:288–289).

Originally planning to retreat by rail, Gen Stilwell had to start north in a convoy because of a train wreck. Finding travel by road virtually impossible and the Japanese slowly encompassing his position, Stilwell abandoned his vehicles and set out for India on foot. With the monsoons soon due to begin, he managed to get his men, now only numbering a few more than a hundred, to the Chindwin River. Here he made a perilous crossing and drove on across the steep, arboreous mountains, finally arriving in Imphal, India, during a pouring rain on 19 May 1942. The monsoons had abated just long enough. Stilwell summed up his feelings while offering a challenge in this manner: ". . . we got a hell of a beating. We got run out of Burma and it is humiliating as hell. I think we ought to find out what caused it, go back and retake it." (26:293–300)

As the monsoon season started in 1942, the Japanese juggernaut had run the King's Own from the rice paddies and teakwood forests of Burma. Japan had cut the overland road to China, she had fortified her land conquests to the east of Burma, and India lay temptingly to the west. The Japanese had overcome all of the defensive obstacles of Burma within the time limits of the impending monsoons. The British had failed to realize the advantages of the bush; to the contrary, the Japanese had employed them to perfection. Now the Japanese used the natural barriers of Burma to establish her defense. The Japanese were thus firmly entrenched in Burma; her troops were fanned out in a border defense that effectively barricaded the door to Southeast Asia.

For the defeated British troops, there was despair; not only because of the humiliating trek back to India, but also for the memory of encounters in the deep, dark primeval rain forests. As related in one soldier's account:

> Unlike the campaigns in Italy and Normandy . . . the very nature of the country in Burma dictated that brutal hand-to-hand clashes decided the outcome of countless encounters. Gloomily we sensed that, inevitably, our future lay in the jungles of Burma and our nightmares contained grinning Japanese, ready to open fire at us from cunningly concealed ambush positions. It was to take a considerable time before we ceased to think of the Japanese soldier as a superman, ten feet tall . . . (22:10, 12).

But even as the last stragglers of the British Army returned to India, a former artillery officer was already studying the contours, rivers, jungles, and situation in Burma to answer the challenge of Gen Stilwell. To mount an offensive, he would have to overcome the terrain, fear, and organizational malaise shown during the Japanese conquest of Burma. Recognizing these factors, this lone figure's unorthodox mind began to scheme and conceive of a bold and unprecedented operation. His plan would ultimately plant the seed for the formulation of a totally new concept in military history. To take back the wedge, springboard, and shield, he would have to beat the Japanese at their own game (38:1).

Chapter Two

WINGATE'S PLAN: THE INCOMPLETE SOLUTION

As soon as British Col Orde C. Wingate arrived in India on 19 March 1942, he, by visiting the Burmese front and flying over the countryside, plunged into an intense and comprehensive evaluation of the situation (32:112). Col Wingate quickly began studying the training and tactics of the Japanese, the religion and customs of Burma and Japan, the climate and topography, and every available report on Japanese fighting in Burma (18:32). He agreed with India Command's assessment; the invincible Chin Hills and Japanese troop emplacements prevented a standard frontal attack. Contrary to commonly held beliefs though, Wingate felt strongly the British soldier could equal the Japanese in the rain forests because of the attribute of imagination.

To overcome the enemy's stranglehold on Burma, Col Wingate theorized the enemy should never know British intentions or strength. Additionally, he felt the British army should present the Japanese with unconventional situations whenever possible (6:138). Slowly he constructed the concept of Long-Range Penetration (LRP) in his mind. At first just a collection of ideas, later Wingate talked incessantly about organizing a force to employ hit-and-run tactics well behind Japanese lines in Burma.

Although there were many disbelievers on India Command's staff, Col Wingate's ideas caught the imagination of Gen Alexander who instructed Wingate to complete the plan. However, because it was innovative and unconventional, LRP actually evolved in stages. To understand the development, an examination of the conception, execution, and evolution stages is dictated.

During his 1942 study of Burma, Wingate concluded although the combination of Burma's wilderness and Japanese perimeter defense could not be assaulted head on, they still were exploitable. Noting Imperial troops were strung out with only a thin supply line connecting them to the interior, Col Wingate proposed an offensive to weaken Japan's grip on Burma based on three principles:

(1) The light concentration of Japanese troops in the core of Burma,
(2) Use of surprise and mobility, and
(3) Employment of aerial firepower and resupply.

Simply stated, Wingate's theory of LRP was to place highly mobile forces in the enemy's rear to harass Japanese lines of communication and destroy supplies. Reminiscent of Confederate Lt Gen Nathan Bedford Forrest's raids during the American War Between the States, Col Wingate proposed an offensive based on the indirect approach. Crucial to his operation would be maneuver; therefore, resupply and artillery were to be provided by air power (31:41).

The Japanese defensive posture after the 1942 offensive pointed to the soft underbelly of the dragon. Wingate stated the enemy was most vulnerable far behind the front where Japanese troops were of inferior quality. Here, he reasoned, a small force could wreak havoc out of all proportion to its number (24:367-368). The size and composition of each group would vary with conditions, the governing principle being strength enough to cause damage yet small enough to slip through the enemy's net. Operations and movements would be conducted during the day; if dispersed, rendezvous would always be made after dark.

The consequence of successful LRP would be widespread confusion and uncertainty behind the enemy's forward areas, leading to progressive weakening and misdirection of the Japanese main forces (41:1). Col Wingate insisted LRP units were not to fight on the front lines and must be used only in conjunction with a major offensive (27:62-74). If a major offensive did not occur, LRP would focus, not redirect, the Japanese forces and the small LRP bands would be annihilated by the full force of the Nippon troops.

Figure 4. Orde C. Wingate

LRP units were not strong enough to withstand the main force; their great strength emerged from mobility. LRP groups would strike, disappear, and turn up somewhere else without the enemy being able to follow their movements through the jungle. The choice of engagement would be dictated by the commander of the LRP group with the objective of LRP being to hit the confluence of supply and communication lines (27:62–74). If LRP units struck a railroad bridge at dawn and a supply dump in the afternoon, the Japanese would be unable to guess the true strength of the columns and probably overestimate their numbers. Furthermore, if two LRP units worked in unison, they could utterly confuse the enemy. Wingate wrote, "Long-Range Penetration affords greater opportunity of mystifying and misleading the enemy than any other form of warfare." (41:1) At the root of Col Wingate's theory of penetration was the value of one fighting man deep in the heart of enemy territory.

Col Wingate further theorized the only limit to the number of fighting men and length of their operations was the availability of supplies. He called this the air support factor. LRP theory proposed air power be used in two ways:

(1) As a flexible supply line and
(2) As airborne artillery and tanks (27:142–147).

This departure from recognized methods of warfare called for the use of portable communications to maintain contact with base camps and detached columns. Wingate could not rely on normal supply lines, so as he colorfully stated, "Have no Lines of Communication on the jungle floor. Bring in the goods like Father Christmas, down the chimney." (9:164) The dropping of supplies was nothing new, nevertheless, the degree of accuracy required did present problems. For this reason, he requested Royal Air Force (RAF) flying officers be assigned to each ground unit to direct aircraft to drop zones and to mark targets in forward areas.

This notion was complicated and time consuming because RAF procedures did not allow direct outside communication with British pilots. Further limiting the effectiveness was the lack of British air superiority over Burma (5:461). Even with this drawback and the complex communication scheme, the plan was submitted to Gen Alexander and forwarded to India Command.

Despite the audacity of the strategy, Gen Wavell supported the plan totally. He included it as a part of a coordinated offensive called ANAKIM. The fulcrum of the plan called for the capture of the airfield at Akyab Island. From Akyab, the British could increase the security of the Bay of Bengal, thereby relieving the pressure on Burma and China from the Japanese Navy and Air Force. If this security could be realized, Gen Wavell felt the reconquest of all of Burma was possible.

The details of the ANAKIM plan involved coordination among a variety of military units, British and Chinese. The plan was as follows:

(1) In mid-October 1942, 15th Corps would mount an offensive into the Arakan region to recapture the port of Akyab;

(2) Amphibious strikes at strategic points along the Arakan coast would supplement the 15th Corps offensive;

(3) Ultimately joining forces, the amphibious units and 15th Corps would continue their attack to Rangoon;

(4) In late January 1943, 4th Corps, commanded by Lt Gen A. F. P. Christison, would launch an assault on the Burmese towns of Sittaung and Kalewa;

(5) The Chinese Ramgarh Force under Gen Stilwell would move south to engage the Japanese at Myitkyina, Bhamo, and Lashio; and

(6) The LRP group would infiltrate the central portion of Burma to confuse and disrupt Japanese lines of communication (24:384; 11:2).

Col Wingate's role in the plan would help secure Northern Burma from the Japanese. As the British advanced, a new road from Ledo would be built to connect with the Burma Road, thus reopening the supply line to China (19:229).

To seal his support of Wingate's plan, in June Gen Wavell established the 77th Indian Infantry Brigade expressly for LRP and promoted Col Wingate to Brigadier General (18:32). In July, assembled in the jungle country around Saugor, Gen Wingate began preparing his troops for the mission to come. His command, certainly not handpicked men, consisted of the following units:

(1) 13th Kings Liverpool Regiment
(2) 3/2nd Gurkha Rifles
(3) 142nd Commando Company
(4) 2nd Burma Rifles
(5) Mule transport company
(6) RAF liaison officers
(7) Officers from the Bush Warfare School at Maymao, Burma (27:63).

Little did Wingate know as he assembled his troops that he would be forced to alter his original mission. Because of the continuing disunity within Gen Wavell's command, Gen Wingate would execute his plan without the primary requirement of LRP—the support of a major offensive.

As Wingate prepared to turn a defeated army into jungle fighters, he devised training methods that were physical, exacting, and thorough. The regime was described by one of the officers as follows: "Every movement, from stand to stand, was done at the double. . . . When he [Wingate] wished to move to another viewpoint, he ran there, and jolly fast too." (24:376)

At first, the strain of the intensive training program took its toll. Before, during, and after the monsoons, Gen Wingate's men were swimming rivers, marching long miles, navigating through the jungle, climbing trees, and scaling hills. Within two months, up to 70 percent of the troops had been in the hospital with real and imaginary cases of malaria, dysentery, and jungle sores (3:35–40). Wingate's reaction was severe but logical. He instituted strict punishments for imaginary illnesses. Further, he eliminated hospital excuses by having all officers instructed on the treatment of illnesses. He reasoned in the jungle, there would be no hospitals and very few medics (27:72–73). The cure slowly showed results as the men hardened under the discipline.

In addition to physical preparedness, Gen Wingate also trained his men in LRP principles; he did this by extensively using a technique called Tactical Exercises without Troops. Normally this involved sand tables modeled into miniature terrain maps. Wingate, insisting on extreme detail, had huge 400-square-yard pits dug so that all enemy troop strengths, as well as pertinent hills, rivers, roads, and gun emplacements, could be depicted to scale. For hours, the officers practiced a spectrum of scenarios envisioned by Gen Wingate: ambush, attack in position, attack while moving a column, use of light artillery, air resupply methods, and dispersion/rendezvous procedures (18:32–36).

Most importantly, he taught his soldiers the security and shelter of the jungle. He demonstrated with maps and aerial photographs that closeness to the enemy did not automatically mean contact. Rather than an enemy, Wingate proposed that the jungle, at the least, was neutral.

Just prior to the scheduled offensive in January 1943, Gen Wingate moved his men forward by hiking 133 miles from the railhead in Dimapur to Imphal. During this march, Wingate administered the last operational test. Departing without rations, he arranged for supplies to be dropped to his columns at prearranged sites after dark (3:38–43). After an 8-day march, he bivouacked outside the town of Imphal, still requiring the brigade to attend long and concentrated lectures. These classroom exercises proved necessary as Gen Wingate's mission was markedly changing even at this late date.

Little by little, the fabric of ANAKIM unravelled, leaving only the 77th Indian Brigade as a participant. First, in late October 1942, Gen Wavell recommended ANAKIM be moved back to November 1943 and a more modest plan be substituted. The new plan, called RAVENOUS, did not include an amphibious operation and it only sought to retake Northern Burma (19:232). Next, 4th Corps cancelled its operation in the Ledo area because of transportation and roadmaking material shortages (24:382). Then, Generalissimo Chaing Kai-shek joined the parade by refusing to participate and withdrew the commitment of his Chinese forces to the operation (5:460).

To make matters worse, in late January 1943, 15th Corps encountered stiff Japanese opposition in the Arakan and stalled. They were never able to advance further and were subsequently driven back! (1:241–243; 46:32–34) In view of the facts, Field Marshall Wavell (DOR:1 January 1943) decided to disband the LRP forces and thus terminate the last vestiges of the operation.

To Field Marshall Wavell's surprise, Gen Wingate resisted. Although the primary prerequisite of a coordinated major offensive was lacking, Wingate argued for an opportunity to test his plan. After prolonged discussions, Field Marshall Wavell finally agreed to a new expedition named Operation LONG-CLOTH. In allowing Gen Wingate's excursion, Field Marshall Wavell let stand the specific tasks of the RAVENOUS plan. The goals given Wingate and his men were as follows:

(1) To cut the main railway line between Mandalay and Myitkyina,
(2) To harass the Shwebo area, and
(3) If possible, cross the Irrawaddy River and sever the railway between Mandalay and Lashio (10:309–310).

After two days of intense planning, Gen Wingate was ready to test LRP principles in actual combat against the Japanese.

A chronology of Operation LONGCLOTH demonstrated the astuteness of Wingate's LRP principles in action. Between 8-10 February, nearly 3,000 men crossed the Chindwin River into Burma (24:388). Unable to cover much distance in the dense undergrowth of the jungle, the columns moved slowly toward the railroad lines near Shwebo. Based on RAF liaison officer inputs, clearings were selected along the way for air drops. On 24, 25, and 26 February, the first series of drops were accomplished (24:395). The results were satisfactory although response time was predictably long.

Shortly after the first airdrops, the brigade's reliance on wireless communications was shown when two of Gen Wingate's columns were ambushed and lost their radios. Without means of communication, the commanders had no other choice than to return to India (24:398–399).

Even with these losses, by 6 March the 77th Indian Brigade had blown up more than 75 sections of the Mandalay-Myitkyina railroad between Shwebo and Wuntho. Field Marshall Wavell's first two tasks were accomplished according to plan and with very little loss of personnel. The Irrawaddy River was now between Wingate and the successful completion of Operation LONGCLOTH.

When Gen Wingate crossed the Irrawaddy, he obliquely proved many of the premises of LRP; in doing so, he almost lost his brigade. With the activity around Shwebo, the Japanese were now fully aware of 77th Indian Brigade's position and turned their full attention on them. The Japanese slowly established a

Figure 5. Northern Burma 1943.

pincer movement that drove Wingate toward an area where the Shweli River formed a loop. Herded into the apex of a triangle with the river on two sides, the force was weakened by the RAF's inability to keep up air resupply (24:412–424).

India Command responded by recommending Gen Wingate terminate the operation and return to India; Wingate concurred without hesitation. His men had reached the point of exhaustion, were no longer receiving supplies, and had begun eating pack mules, snakes, and rats. Casualties had also become a major problem. Unable to keep up with the rapidly moving columns, injured men were often left at Burmese villages or under the shade of a tree with nothing more than a canteen of water, a rifle, and, sometimes, the Bible (64:—). To withdraw the rest of his troops, Gen Wingate had no options; he recrossed the Irrawaddy River on the night of 27 March (24:418–419).

Unable to shake his Japanese pursuers, Wingate finally issued the order for the force to form dispersion groups and work their way back to India or China. The escape worked as diagrammed despite Japanese constant harassment (27:54–94). One group, led by Maj Walter P. Scott, even enticed a C-47 into landing in a small jungle clearing and airlifting 17 wounded soldiers to safety (30:23–24).

Not all the others were so lucky. Operation LONGCLOTH lasted from 8 February until early June; of the 3,000 who entered Burma, only 2,182 returned to India but most were unfit for future combat (10:324). Notwithstanding these heavy losses and despite suffering from exhaustion, when the 77th Indian Brigade finally reached safety in India their spirits were high (6:140).

Gen Wingate's troops had reason to feel good about Operation LONGCLOTH. The mission had dealt a blow to the Japanese and proved a number of elements of LRP theory. LRP was actually able to exploit Japanese weaknesses in the interior of Burma; the successful raids on the railroads amply demonstrated this fact. Secondly, LRP's mobility and surprise had confused the Japanese for nearly two months. It was only when air resupply was unable to respond quickly enough to Wingate's needs that the mission broke down. Because of similarly slow responses, the brigades never exploited the firepower aspect of the theory.

Gen Wingate's operation brought to light the strengths and weaknesses of LRP operations. Wingate had overcome Burma's terrain and the residual fear from the Japanese invasion, but he did not get the organizational support necessary for complete victory. LRP was never intended to be the primary, let alone sole, operation; its value was to divide the attention of the enemy. Operation LONGCLOTH simply violated its own principles and the Japanese were finally able to corral the operation and pick it apart. What Gen Wingate did not foresee was the most devastating weakness; his inability to evacuate the wounded had a grave effect on morale. The later events of the operation did not detract from the mission's overall value though. For the first time, British troops had fought a jungle war against the Japanese and had delivered punishment. In Wingate's words, "a weapon has been found which may well prove a counter to the obstinate but unimaginative courage of the Japanese soldier." (46:24)

On 21 May, the *London Daily Times* released the invasion story for world-wide dissemination. During this report, the name Chindit was given to the 77th Indian Brigade. Gen Wingate explained the term described a mythological beast, half-lion and half-griffin. Portrayed as statutes which guard Burmese pagodas, the lion-griffin symbolized to Wingate the unique cooperation required between ground and air forces (18:19). The description captured the imagination of Englishmen around the globe. The British press was extremely favorable in its treatment of the Chindits; their success contrasted sharply with the failure of 15th Corps' Arakan operation. Because of the publicity, Gen Wingate became the British champion of Burma (27:93).

Additionally, the exploits of the Chindits fired the hope and praise of the Allies (6:149). A look at the circumstances and effect of the mission shows its impact on future Burma operations.

Prior to the Chindit mission, US and British planners had been at loggerheads about Burma. Since the Japanese had closed all overland supply routes to China in early 1942, US air power, flying over the Himalayas, kept provisions of fuel and materiel flowing into Chiang Kai-shek. However, increased Japanese actions required more stores than feasible using the "Hump" resupply method. US planners realized that if China was unable to hold out against the 20-odd Japanese divisions on their mainland, these experienced units could be released to fight elsewhere in the Pacific (13:6). US President Roosevelt, considering China a cornerstone in the war against Japan, wanted the Burma Road reopened.

Britain's Prime Minister Churchill, on the other hand, was more concerned with maintaining the British Empire. Because China had territorial claims on Northern Burma, Churchill wanted a weak China to emerge from the war (26:369–370). Based on these two interconnected priorities, the Prime Minister was not interested in relieving China's supply problems. Britain consistently recommended an amphibious assault in Sumatra with a push toward the recapture of Singapore.

President Roosevelt's trump card was to tie US demands for a Burma offensive to Britain's greatest need, war machinery. The inability of Britain to demonstrate a successful strategy to re-secure the Burma Road had been a source of embarassment to Churchill and his planning staff. To pump some life into India Command, the Prime Minister's staff was proposing the establishment of Southeast Asia Command (SEAC) to coordinate the complex interlocking and overlapping areas of command, geography, and operations (26:383). A new organization, however, was not a strategy. When he witnessed the press reaction to the Chindits, Churchill realized he had a new means of surmounting the topographic defenses of Burma and a new champion in Gen Wingate.

In July, Churchill called Wingate back to London to discuss the Chindit LRP operations. After speaking to Gen Wingate, the Prime Minister invited him to attend the upcoming Quadrant Conference in Quebec, Canada. The purpose of Quadrant was to establish overall Allied strategy, and although it primarily dealt with the European Theater, operations in Burma were to be discussed.

Specifically, Churchill wanted Wingate "to explain his recent operation with a long-range penetration group and to set out his views on their future employment." (41:1) During the conference, Gen Wingate proposed to expand the number of units, in steps, to eight brigade groups for the forthcoming 1943–44 dry season offensive. Four of the units would lead the operation while four would be held in reserve. Wingate felt LRP units should only be subjected to combat for 90-day periods before

Figure 6. Chindit: Derivative of Burmese Chinthe.

25

being relieved for a rest. In addition to LRP units, a major offensive would be mounted with the following objectives:

(1) The occupation of Bhamo and Lashio,
(2) The occupation of Katha-Indaw airfield and a drive toward Pinlebu and Kalewa, and
(3) An assault from Ledo toward Myitkina.

Gen Wingate's fortified LRP groups would act in coordination with British and Chinese forces whose overall objective was limited to the conquest of Burma north of the 23rd Parallel (41:1).

Gen Wingate's Quadrant plan also included requirements for aircraft support. He asked for approximately 16 DC-3 aircraft for airdrop and an allotment of one bomber squadron per unit for close air support (41:2). Additionally, at the insistence of one of his RAF liaison officers, Squadron Leader Robert "Tommy" Thompson, Gen Wingate sought to overcome previous morale problems by requesting a "Light Plane Force" to assist in the evacuation of wounded LRP personnel (34:8). The US reaction to a plan to reopen the Burma Road was viewed favorably.

While offering Wingate's LRP plan to secure Northern Burma, the British were forced to request American assistance. With the constant demands on war materiel in Europe, the British supply capability was overcommitted resulting in the China-Burma-India (CBI) Theater having the lowest priority in the war. Food was a critical item and equipment, such as weapons, vehicles, planes, and medicine, was always in short supply (21:140–154). Britain simply could not meet all the demands of Gen Wingate's Quadrant plan. Prime Minister Churchill felt that England had the necessary bombers, but he was unable to provide the following requirements:

(1) Two LRP brigades,
(2) The DC-3 Dakotas, and
(3) The evacuation aircraft.

At the Quadrant Conference, the Prime Minister had Gen Wingate brief President Roosevelt; then when he had the President's agreement on the mission, Churchill followed up the briefing with a request for American men and materiel.

The President endorsed Wingate's bold strategy and forwarded Churchill's petition for help through channels. The request for aircraft went to US General of the Army Henry H. (Hap) Arnold for action. Because of Arnold's experience with airpower, his fertile mind saw more in the plan than simple light airplanes. Like Churchill, Arnold wanted to put new life in the CBI Theater because he felt the previous campaigns had sapped the will of the British ground troops. In his mind, Arnold saw an opportunity to exploit and expand airpower. He became determined to form a new air organization which would be totally dedicated to supporting Wingate's troops on the ground in Burma (56:143, 149). The successful realization of that strategy rested in Arnold's choice of a commander to breathe life into his vision.

Chapter Three

1ST AIR COMMANDO GROUP: THE TOOL

On 26 August 1943, newly named Supreme Allied Commander of SEAC, British Adm Lord Louis Mountbatten met with Gen Arnold to discuss plans for the CBI Theater. During this discussion, Adm Mountbatten reportedly brought up the idea of enlarging on Gen Wingate's mission (27:246). Gen Arnold restated his support of LRP and committed his plan to develop an autonomous organization for this purpose. Gen Arnold's conception of this new force was as a highly mobile fighting unit complete with its own transportation and services. It would be an experiment looking toward future air warfare (61:1). As the unit evolved, it would change names five times. The evolution was as follows:

(1) Project 9,
(2) Project CA 281,
(3) 5318th Provisional Unit (Air),
(4) No. 1 Air Commando Force, and
(5) 1st Air Commando Group (62:November/December 1983:6)

Arnold's first priority was to find men who would infuse the US "can-do" spirit into the CBI Theater. Having formed other "specials" and monitored their operations, Gen Arnold had concerns. Too often he had seen theater organizations absorb these unique forces, causing them to fail their purpose. Therefore, the selection of commander was critical as he would ultimately decide the composition, morale, and employment of the unit. Gen

Arnold requested members of his staff nominate candidates for command of this experimental organization; five nominations were finally submitted. In a short period of time, the search narrowed to two individuals (56:143–144).

The first, Lt Col Philip G. Cochran, fit Gen Arnold's desired qualities; he was confident, aggressive, imaginative, and had a highly distinguished war record as a fighter pilot in Africa. In November 1942, then-Maj Cochran had led a group of 35 replacement pilots and planes to North Africa. Informed that casualties were lighter than expected, Cochran determined his men were not needed. Without headquarters sanction, he took the pilots to Rabat, Morocco, named them the Joker Squadron, and began training for combat. When the Joker Squadron was discovered, headquarters ordered it back to Casablanca. However, Cochran and seven of his fellow aviators were sent to Tunisia to reinforce the remnants of two P-40 squadrons. Upon reporting to the airfield near the Kasserine Pass, Maj Cochran noted he was the ranking officer and took over the 58th Squadron. Forced to live in caves because of their proximity to the front, 58th Squadron personnel concentrated on attacking Axis truck and train routes to relieve pressure on French and American forces. Because of the success of Cochran's raids, the Germans were forced to begin moving supplies by night and hiding trucks under haystacks during the day. However, this tactic did not slow down Cochran's men; they began attacking haystacks with outstanding results! Among his missions was one in which Cochran loaded a P-40 with two 500-pound bombs and blew up the heavily defended German headquarters at Kairouan (29:42–48; 58:10–11).

After six months of combat, Cochran had downed two German fighters and won the Distinguished Flying Cross with two clusters, a Silver Star, the Soldier's Medal, the Air Medal with three clusters, and the Croix de Guerre with Star and Palm (39:Cochran Interview). Unknown to Gen Arnold, Lt Col Cochran was also the model for the character of Flip Corkin in Milton Caniff's "Terry and the Pirates" comic strip (29:42–48; 58:10–11).

Although Gen Arnold did not know Cochran, he recognized the name of the second candidate, Lt Col John R. Alison. Like Cochran, Alison represented qualities desired by Gen Arnold, although the qualities were not the same. Alison was tactful, well

Figure 7. Philip G. Cochran.

organized, a consummate pilot with a superb flying record, and experienced in the Far East. A 1936 Engineering School graduate from the University of Florida, Alison drew on his technical training during one of his first assignments: administering the sensitive US-Russian lend-lease program of P-40 aircraft. Dispatched to Russia during the summer of 1941 by Harry Hopkins, trusted advisor of President Roosevelt, Alison was charged with reassembling the crated planes upon delivery at the Arctic port of Arkhangelsk. As the planes began to arrive, Capt Hubert (Hub) Zemke, later of the famous "Wolfpack" Squadron, joined the program as the Chief of Operations; he and Alison then began teaching Russian pilots to operate the American warplanes. Without technical orders, they put together P-40 Tomahawks and tested every one prior to delivery. When the numbing Russian winter shut down operations, the State Department allowed Zemke to leave, but Capt Alison stayed on as the Assistant Military Attache for Air. Finally in January 1942, Alison secured a verbal release from Gen George C. Marshall's special emissary to the Soviet Union, Lt Col Townsen Griffiths. (57:13–29)

Alison left Russia and travelled to Basra, Iraq, believing Griffiths would forward written orders upon returning to Washington. The orders never came. Finally in April, Alison tragically learned Griffiths' plane had been shot down over the English Channel. Officially, Alison had been AWOL for over three months! Meanwhile he had attached himself to a small engineering unit which was assisting the British as they received lend-lease A-20s. Even though he had not flown the aircraft, Alison took charge of the operation and cabled the War Department to inform them of his new duties. Duplicating the program in Russia, Alison periodically forwarded pencil-written progress reports directly to Gen Arnold, always with a postscript requesting combat duty when relieved. (57:32–35; 63:—)

In June 1942, he was finally sent to the China Theater as a pilot for US MGen Claire L. Chennault's 23rd Fighter Group, known previously as the American Volunteer Group (AVG) "Flying Tigers." During this tour, Alison organized the first successful night interception of Japanese airplanes. After shooting down two Mitsuibishi Type 97 bombers, Alison's plane was hit and he had to make a forced landing in the Siang Kiang River, a tributary of the Yangtze. Later, he became an ace by downing

Figure 8. John R. Alison.

six enemy aircraft and was one of a select few US pilots who flew a captured Japanese Zero. Lt Col Alison returned to the US in May 1943 and was training the 367th Fighter Group on the West Coast when Gen Arnold summoned him for an interview (38:7; 57:—).

During the interviews, Gen Arnold hoped to find a man to lead his unique organization who was aggressive, imaginative, and highly organized (28:129). Together, Cochran and Alison possessed these qualities. Cochran was cavalier, outspoken, a positive leader, and possessed an innovative mind. By contrast, Alison was disciplined, articulate, a quiet leader, and had demonstrated a diplomatic demeanor. Unable to make a clear selection, Gen Arnold explained the details of the project separately to Cochran and Alison. After the operation was outlined, each man stated his opposition, thinking of it only as a light plane evacuation organization. Playing "Alphonse and Gaston," each tried to persuade Gen Arnold to give the job to the other (56:144–147).

Gen Arnold solved the problem by naming them co-commanders, adding that there was more to the project than met the eye. Gen Arnold said, "I not only want you to [take out the wounded] . . . but I want the USAAF to spearhead General Wingate's operation." (42:3) Gen Arnold then terminated the session by saying, "To hell with the paper work, go out and fight." (28:130) Perhaps not intending them to take him literally, Cochran and Alison did just that after setting up offices in the Pentagon and the Hay-Adams House, a Washington hotel.

Trying to better understand LRP and the mission of the new unit, Lt Col Cochran immediately flew to England to talk to Adm Mountbatten and Gen Wingate (56:152). During discussions about the previous campaign and long-range penetration theory, Cochran began to formulate the organization of Gen Arnold's vision, known at the time as Project 9.

After talking with Wingate, Cochran enlarged his concept of the mission of Project 9. Based on the 1943 Chindit campaign and focusing on the LRP principle of air support, Cochran and Alison decided to take on the responsibility for all of Wingate's air requirements. They began "building a whole small region of warfare where we had ground troops, artillery, infantry, air-ground support, fighter support, and bombardment support." (56:157–158)

There was no table of organization for a unit of this kind, so Cochran and Alison used their imagination to determine the structure and personnel requirements. They were able to get what they wanted because "Gen Arnold had given them practically carte blanche orders to gather men and materiel under the highest priority." (60:1) Among the first personnel assignments to Project 9 were Maj Samson Smith as Executive Officer; Maj Arvid E. Olson, a former AVG pilot, as Operations Officer; and Capt Charles L. Engelhardt as Administrative Assistant (48:4). Later, Capt Robert E. Moist was added as the organization's Adjutant. The Project 9 group immediately launched into manning the unit. Due to the classification of the project, interested personnel were told only a minimum amount of information. Not advised of the destination, applicants were assured the mission included combat, the time period involved would be no more than six months, all who joined would be volunteers, and personnel should expect no promotions. At the Quadrant Conference, the RAF had agreed to supply the bomber requirement; therefore, the co-commanders were seeking volunteers for three major types of aircraft—fighters, transports, and light planes.

To provide air support to LRP units, Cochran and Alison proposed an assault force of fighters. The fighter section, working directly with the Chindits, would fully test Wingate's theory of airborne artillery. The lure of combat duty and the secret nature of Project 9 made recruiting simple. Cochran said, "[W]e were allowed to bring in from anywhere—if we knew [a] man's name, we'd send for him. We knew them through our time in the Air Force." (56:161) Cochran and Alison selected Maj Grant Mahony to lead the fighter section. He had combat experience throughout the Pacific, was an ace (five kills), and had flown with Lt Col Alison in China. Maj Robert T. Smith, also an ace (eight kills) and a former AVG pilot, was selected as his deputy. After the unit was deployed to India, Maj Robert L. Petit, winner of a Silver Star for air battles at Guadalcanal, replaced Maj Smith (36:179–180; 66:—). As pilots were brought into the unit, they recommended others. Crew chiefs and enlisted men who had previously served under the leaders were asked to join the unit.

For aircraft, Project 9 recommended P-38 Lightnings for the

close air support requirements (60:2). When this request was denied, the co-commanders substituted P-47 Thunderbolts and requested an allocation of 30 aircraft (41:Memorandum from Arnold to Marshall).

For the transport requirements, Cochran and Alison determined a need for three separate units. They decided to recruit pilots for transport, glider, and light-cargo airplanes. Each would fill a distinct role in the organization.

The mission of the transport section was to provide responsive airland and airdrop support for the Chindits. Maj William T. Cherry, Jr., pilot of E. V. (Eddie) Rickenbacker's ill-fated Pacific trip, was selected to command this section. Capt Jacob B. Sartz, who earlier had bombed the Japanese from a C-87, the cargo version of a B-24 and flew 72 refugees on one of the last Dakotas out of Rangoon in 1942, was chosen to be his deputy (36:179–180; 60:1).

To fully support the Chindits, Cochran proposed the use of gliders to transport heavy artillery to LRP units; Alison, likewise, saw the potential for gliders to resupply Wingate by moving men and equipment into small jungle clearings which could not otherwise be accessed (56:158). At the recommendation of the Pentagon, Capt William H. Taylor, Jr. and 1Lt Vincent Rose were respectively selected Glider Section commander and deputy. Once assigned, Capt Taylor hand-picked all glider pilots and mechanics for the unit from Bowman Field in Louisville, Kentucky (43:1).

Because Project 9 was designed as a self-contained fighting unit, Alison recognized a requirement for a light-cargo aircraft to provide unit support. Lt Col Clinton B. Gaty was selected from Wright Field to command the light-cargo section because, as an engineer, he could do more than just fly. Cochran related, "[He was a] guy to head up our whole maintenance-engineering function, to take care of [our] aircraft in the jungle, to practically rebuild them if we had to." (56:165) Capt Edward Wagner was selected to assist Lt Col Gaty.

The Project 9 team recommended 13 C-47 Dakotas for the aircraft requirements of the transport section. The glider section requested 100 CG-4A Waco gliders, capable of carrying 15 troopers, and 25 TG-5 training gliders for use in remote sites. For unit support, Project 9 selected a little known "bush" airplane used extensively in Canada, the UC-64 Noorduyn Norseman.

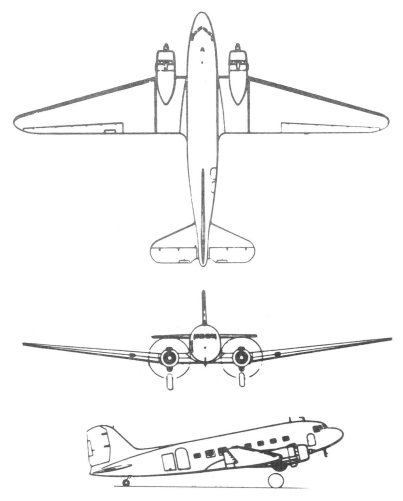

Figure 9. C–47 Dakota (Skytrain).

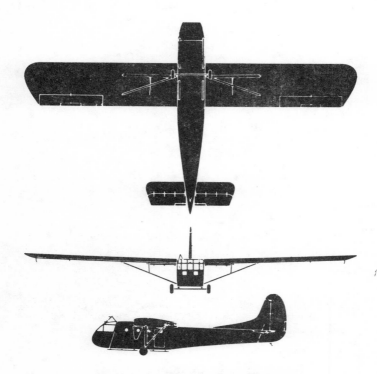

Figure 10. CG–4A Waco Glider.

38

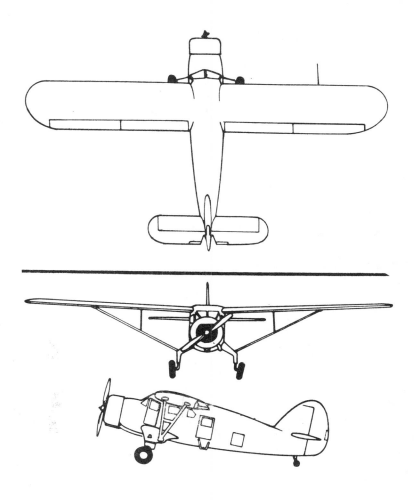

Figure 11. UC-64 Norseman.

With a ceiling of 17,000 feet, a top speed of 160 mph, and a capability of carrying 2,000 pounds; the 12 requested Norsemen were ticketed to be a bridge between the C-47 and the light planes planned for medical evacuation (62:May/June 1985:6).

The light planes were not only to be used for the evacuation of wounded; they were also to provide liaison and transport of light supplies between India and the forward lines. The light planes would be flown almost entirely by enlisted pilots. At the recommendation of Capt Taylor, Maj Andrew P. Rebori was chosen to command the liaison section, and he, in turn, brought along Capt Everett F. Smith as his deputy. Because Project 9 was to be a mobile unit, Maj Rebori required volunteers be trained in at least one useable craft other than aviation. Electricians and mechanics were essential in the CBI because the pilots would be expected to fix their own planes (68:—).

For the light plane force, Maj Rebori selected the L-1 Vigilant. The plane carried two to three stretchers behind the pilot and had a short takeoff roll. Maj Rebori required 100 L-1 Vigilants; however, when the number of serviceable aircraft could not be located, he augmented the L-1 with the newer L-5 Sentinel (60:2). The Sentinels were faster than the L-1; however, they were designed to seat only one evacuee. The L-5 was also less desired because its technical data called for a much longer runway—about 900 feet (48:6).

In addition to the light planes, Cochran and Alison decided to employ the newly developed helicopter in Burma. Cochran placed the diplomatic Alison in charge of securing the pre-production model YR-4 for rescue service in the jungle. Although he was initially turned down, Alison finally persuaded Wright Field to send a technical representative to India to test four of Sikorsky's unproven helicopters in actual combat (63:—).

The organization, insofar as equipment was concerned, was equal to a USAAF wing carrying a normal complement of about 2,000 men (60:2). Because of time constraints though, Project 9 personnel had to be completely air transported. Therefore, the requirements—including medical, supply, engineering, intelligence, and communication sections—were kept lean: 87 officers and 436 enlisted men (41:Memorandum from Gen Arnold to Gen Marshall, 13 September 1943).

Lt Col Cochran and Lt Col Alison sent their planned organi-

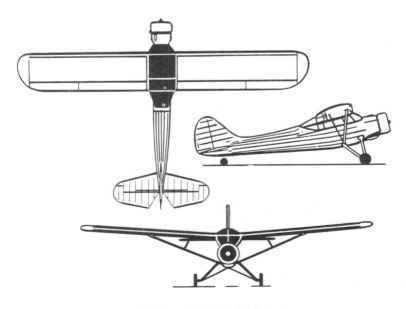

Figure 12. L–1 Vigilant.

Figure 13. L–5 Sentinel.

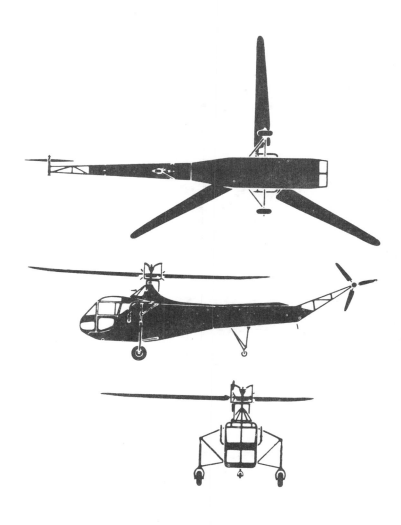

Figure 14. YR–4 Helicopter.

43

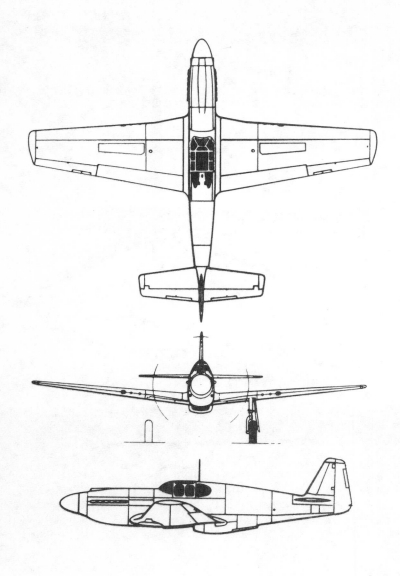

Figure 15. P-51A Mustang.

zation through channels to Gen Arnold who forwarded his approval to General of the Army George Marshall on 13 September 1943. The only alteration to the request involved the fighters; P-51A Mustangs were substituted for the Thunderbolts. In less than 30 days, Cochran and Alison had built themselves a unit and gotten it approved! Their next job was to imbue the unit with life and prepare the personnel for deployment.

As the unit formed, the men seemed to sense they were exceptional and began acting accordingly (56:172–175). Gathering in North Carolina on 1 October—the fighters and gliders at Seymour-Johnson Field and the light planes at Raleigh-Durham—Project 9 began requisitioning specialized equipment. New ideas were encouraged. As a result, a new mobile hospital was included on the required equipment list and blueprints for experimental rocket tubes were ordered from Wright Field for the fighters. The Dakotas were to be equipped with the newest development in glider towing, a reel for airborne aircraft to "snatch" gliders off the ground (60:2). For the gliders, Capt Taylor requested each Waco be equipped with gyro towing devices somewhat similar to an automatic pilot mechanism (37:2). Furthermore, Maj Rebori designed bomb racks so parachute packs could be mounted on the wings of L-1 and L-5 aircraft (48:6). For the men, the co-commanders had convinced the Army to issue weapons to all of the flyers in the unit—Thompson submachine guns, carbines, and .45 automatic pistols. So instead of the normal Port of Embarkation training given to overseas-bound soldiers, Project 9 spent spare time at the rifle range.

In North Carolina, some flight training was also conducted. While the fighter sections assembled and began indoctrination courses on the P-51A and its Allison engine, the gliders got flying time (60:1). The gliders obtained the use of two C-47 "tugs" and crews, one each from the 436th and 439th Troop Carrier Squadrons, and practiced single, double, and automatic tow; airborne glider pick-ups; flying in position below the C-47; and night operations (37:2). Double tow was emphasized to maximize airlift capability. In this method, two gliders, one on a short rope and the other on a longer line, were towed by one C-47. Close coordination between glider pilots and a steady hand by "tug" pilots was required. As a result of their skills, two of the "loaned" C-47 pilots, 2Lt Patrick Driscoll and 2Lt Vincent L. Ulery, were asked to join Project 9.

The light plane pilots also worked with the gliders by towing TG-5 gliders, but primarily they busied themselves learning about their airplanes. Because the L-1 was obsolete and the L-5 was new to the USAAF inventory, most of the "flying sergeants" had not flown either and certainly not under the anticipated conditions in Burma. To simulate jungle obstacles, Maj Rebori stretched ropes across the Raleigh-Durham runway and made the light plane pilots practice short-field landings and take-offs over and over again. In fully loaded aircraft, the pilots began to routinely make takeoffs in 500-600 feet. While airborne, they trained themselves in low level flying. When the townspeople complained about planes flying at 100 feet, Maj Rebori replied they should have been lower! (68:—).

Originally scheduled to embark about 15 December, the group had to curtail the entire training program when the departure date was moved up 45 days (37:1–2). As the embarkation date neared, the enthusiasm of the unit soared. Flight Surgeon Cortez Enloe said, "They had the greatest morale of any outfit I ever saw, but not such strict discipline." (25:106) When the first group to leave Goldsboro was issued gear, complete with ammunition, some of them discharged their weapons in the railroad station while waiting for the train. Bullets were withheld from subsequent groups (60:2). Armed with a transportation priority high enough to "bump" generals, the unit was scheduled to fly from Miami to Karachi, India, by way of Puerto Rico, Trinadad, British Guiana, Brazil, Ascension Island, Gold Coast, Nigeria, Ango-Egyptian Sudan, Aden, and Masira Island (65:—). Ahead of the main unit, Col Cochran was already on his way, leaving Miami on 3 November.

True to his word, Gen Arnold had superimposed the organization on SEAC by forwarding a letter to USAAF MGen George Stratemeyer, a member of Mountbatten's staff and soon to be named commander of the Eastern Air Command. In the letter, dated 13 September, Gen Arnold stated, ". . . the Air Task Force will be assigned to the Commanding General of the United States Army Forces in the China-India-Burma [sic] Theater for administration and supply and operate under the control of the Allied Commander-in-Chief, South-East Asia." Gen Arnold had also carefully defined the purpose of Project 9:

(1) To facilitate the forward movement of the Windgate [sic] columns.

(2) To facilitate the supply and evacuation of the columns.

(3) To provide a small air covering and striking force.

(4) To acquire air experience under the conditions expected to be encountered (41:Memo for Chief of Staff, Subject: Air Task Force Windgate [sic], dated 13 September 1943).

Knowing the mission given him by Gen Arnold, Col Cochran wanted to discuss the latest developments with Adm Mountbatten, find facilities for his personnel and aircraft, and complete the training programs when he arrived in India.

Despite an engine change and a short delay enroute, Cochran and a small group of his men arrived in Western India on 13 November (62:April 1980:2). One of Cochran's first duties was to report to Delhi where Adm Mountbatten had temporarily set up his headquarters.

When Cochran first talked to the SEAC staff, the facts of Gen Arnold's letter were not generally known and changes had been made to the Quadrant Conference plans. As Col Alison later wrote:

When Colonel Cochran arrived in the theater the general plan for Wingate's operation was to march into Burma initially three long-range penetration brigades. One to cross the Chindwin River from the West, one to march down from the North and a third to be flown to China and marched across the Salween to spearhead a Chinese advance. This unit would have to be moved by air to China, then resupplied by air from Chinese bases. [USA] General Stilwell [Deputy Supreme Commander of SEAC] said that because of air lift limitations this would be impossible and the whole plan of offensive operations in Burma for this season were in danger of being abandoned. Colonel Cochran arrived at this meeting where [British] General Auchinleck [Commander-in-Chief in India], General Stilwell, [USAAF] General Chennault [Commander, 14th Air Force], Admiral Mountbatten and General Stratemeyer's representative were present. At this time no-one in the theater, not even Admiral Mountbatten or General Wingate, knew what the 1st Air Commando Group intended to do for Wingate's operation. Colonel Cochran was called upon to explain why we had been sent into the theater and at this meeting he explained to the Chiefs of Staff that it was not necessary to fly the third brigade to China, that the brigade should be streamlined and that the 1st Air Commando Force would move this brigade into the heart of Burma from bases in India. He was asked if this was possible and if it would be possible for the 1st Air Commando Force to move the brigade to the job in two weeks time. He stated that the 1st Air Commandos would do the job in one week or less. At this meeting Admiral Mountbatten made the statement, "Boy, you are the first ray of sunshine we have seen in this theater for some time." (41:Memorandum for General Giles from Col John Alison, 10 Apr 44)

To back up his claim, on 24 November, Cochran cabled Alison, still in the US, requesting an additional 50 GC-4A Waco gliders. Although the mission would remain a constant political football, for now it was back on the front burner. By the following day, the additional gliders had departed the US for India (40:4).

When the unit's aircraft started arriving, Cochran knew he would have to make arrangements for facilities. To expedite the flow of equipment, the C-47 Dakotas were flown over, using basically the same route as the rest of the men. All other airplanes were shipped by sea. The P-51A Mustangs were deck-loaded on carriers; the gliders and all other airplanes were disassembled and crated. With the exception of the gliders, everything was headed for Karachi (60:2–3). Cochran would have to put his airplanes back together before permanently locating the unit.

Col Cochran secured the Karachi Airport dirigible hangar to receive and assemble the unit's airplanes. Unfortunately, just prior to Christmas, two shipments of P-51A Mustangs were received in non-operational condition because of saltwater corrosion and storm damage. Since no replacements were available in the theater, priority spares had to be ordered (40:5). The crated planes faired better. Because of limited personnel, officers and enlisted men pitched in to assemble the UC-64 and L-series planes as the crates were offloaded. Visitors to the site remarked on the unit's spirit of cooperation. On a temporary basis, Project 9 established a headquarters near Karachi at Malir Airfield and the newly christened 5318th Provisional Unit (Air) began training exercises and theater indoctrination (60:3).

On 1 December, the glider section got transportation to Barrackpore Field, near Calcutta, where they began rigging and testing their gliders (30:10). Although all the gliders were supposed to be shipped to Calcutta, on 23 December, Capt Taylor was forced to send four of his personnel back across India to assemble some gliders inadvertently sent to Karachi (49:18). As the gliders were rigged, the pilots would test fly each one for practice and evaluation.

48

Figure 16. Assembling aircraft in dirigible hangar.

On Christmas Eve, after Col Alison arrived, he, Col Cochran, Capt Taylor, and others flew to the Assam region of Northeast India to survey two airfields recommended for their use, Lalaghat and Hailakandi. Maj Robert C. Page, head of the medical section, described the airfields as grass strips, "entirely British in construction. All barracks were basha [native bamboo hut] in type." (60:Medical History:19) The group decided the 6,300-foot strip at Lalaghat would be used by the transports and gliders, and Hailakandi, some 8 to 10 miles away, would be for the fighters and light planes. Located on a tea plantation, Hailakandi was only 4,500 feet long (51:12, 14).

The co-commanders decided Lt Col Gaty would command Lalaghat, and Cochran would run Hailakandi. After Alison's arrival in India, the two had determined that the co-command arrangement was awkward. To simplify matters, officially Col Cochran was deemed the commander and Col Alison took the title of his deputy. They were in such accord, however, that a decision by one automatically became the decision of the other (48:5).

Having found a permanent home, Cochran and Alison were able to turn their full attention to supporting Wingate's 3rd Indian Division, also known as Special Force. It was during this stage of evolution that the 5318th conducted training exercises with the Chindits, enlarged their own assault force, and exploited Gen Arnold's fourth purpose, "to acquire air experience under the conditions expected to be encountered."

During the time that Capt Taylor's men were rigging gliders, they also conducted joint training drills. These operational tests with the Chindits helped cement the bond between the two units.

Flight training practice began on 29 December. Ten days later, a 20-glider day exercise was performed in which 400 men were landed on a mud field at Lalitpur. Even though four gliders did not release, the exercise was pronounced a success. However, there was one problem—the gliders got stuck in the mud and couldn't be moved by ground personnel. To solve the problem and demonstrate the capabilities of the unit, Col Cochran arranged to have the gliders "snatched" out that night and the following morning (37:5).

During one of the day training exercises, the assault force allayed some fears expressed about the evacuation airplanes. 1Lt

Paul G. Forcey, a former RAF pilot assigned to P-51s and the character "Hot Shot" Charlie in Milton Caniff's comic strip, demonstrated the survivability of a L-5 Sentinel to the Chindits and light plane pilots. With Maj Petit flying a Mustang and Lt Forcey in a L-5, the planes squared off in a mock dogfight. Beer bets were made and covered. Using the smaller turn radius of the L-5 to advantage, Forcey continually out-maneuvered the faster aircraft. Gun cameras later verified that Lt Forcey had remained safely out of the kill envelope of Maj Petit's Mustang (66:—).

These exercises helped Special Force and Col Cochran's men work out solutions to each difficulty. For instance, one of the problems Capt Taylor anticipated was the transportaiton of mules. After many suggestions, including dragging the beasts, it was finally decided on the night of 10 January 1944 to see if the animals could be transported without them kicking holes in the side of gliders. For this test, the following precautions were taken: the glider floors were reinforced, the mule's legs were hobbled, their heads were tied down to keep the ears out of the control cables, and they were restricted in a sling-like contraption. Flight Officer Allen Hall, Jr. was selected to fly the glider (49:21). Last minute instructions were given muleteers to shoot the animals if they became unmanageable. The worries were all in vain; the mules performed well, reportedly even banking during turns! (56:238)

Following this night session, Gen Wingate decided to join in the activities and participate in a "snatch." (37:1–3) Adm Mountbatten, who had also attended the night exercise, was impressed with what he saw and discussed expanding the mission with Gen Wingate and Col Cochran. They agreed that an assault group of Chindits and an engineering unit could be towed in gliders to jungle clearings in Burma. Defended against attack by the Chindits, the engineers could then cut out a landing strip for C-47 Dakotas. Once the strip was built, the remainder of Gen Wingate's brigades could be airlanded deep behind enemy lines (37:4–7; 60:25–). Capt Taylor agreed with the concept and continued daily glider training as the remainder of the unit prepared Lalaghat and Hailakandi for business.

To make their airfields operational, the men of the 5318th Provisional Unit repeated the procedures established at Karachi.

Officer and enlisted personnel labored side by side to transfer oil and fuel drums from the railhead at Dimapur to Lalaghat and Hailakandi. Working virtually around the clock, the men of the 5318th were further required to strain the petroleum through chamois skins to remove rust and other impurities. Wearily the men continued the work, disregarding physical hygiene. When BGen William D. Old, Commander of the Troop Carrier Command, made a remark about the slovenliness of the unit, Col Cochran posted a notice that read:

To: All Personnel and Attached Organizations.

Look, Sports, the beards and attempts at beards are not appreciated by visitors.

Since we can't explain to all strangers that the fuzz is a gag, we must avoid their reporting that we are unshaven (regulations say shave) by appearing like Saturday night in Jersey.

Work comes before shaving. You will never be criticized for being unkempt, if you are so damn busy you can't take time to doll-up. But be clean while you can.

Ain't it awful?

P. G. Cochran
Colonel, Air Corps
Commanding (34:23)

The beards came off, the work went on, and reportedly, Gen Old got as greasy as the rest when he pitched in to help! (69:—)

Meanwhile, as the glider training progressed, Capt Taylor decided against the normal 360 degree overhead landing pattern in favor of a more rapid straight-in approach. A release point for the gliders was established 200 yards forward of the landing field. To accommodate two gliders, the field was marked with four lights configured in a diamond, 150 yards on a side. The top and bottom of the diamond divided the landing zone in half. In effect, two landing strips were marked—one on either side of the dividing line between the flanker lights.

Then, on 15 February, a mishap occurred during a night double tow which killed four British and three US troops. The potential pall of the accident was lifted the following day when Gen Wingate's unit commander sent the following note: "Please be assured that we will go with your boys any place, any time, anywhere." (25:155) This phrase captured the degree of teamwork achieved by the British and American groups and was adopted as the motto of the 1st Air Commandos.

By contrast, RAF support to the Chindits was not as well coordinated. That fact, along with the requirement for an engineering unit, was cause for the 5318th Provisional to grow one last time.

The first enlargement occurred when problems developed concerning RAF bomber support to Gen Wingate's columns. The RAF had recently equipped their bombers with radios which were incompatible with those of the Chindits. Col Alison wrote:

> At a conference with the RAF in the Imphal area it became clear that there were differences of opinion concerning the close support of Wingate columns and the mechanical feasibility of direction of assault from the ground. The RAF in this area is committed to the defense of an area, the support of an army and the support of Wingate and from the conversation it appeared that assault support for Wingate would be limited (41:Letter to General H. H. Arnold from Col John Alison, Subject: History, Status and Immediate Requirements for 1st Air Commando Force, 21 January 1944).

Gen Wingate, faced with a repeat of the same slow response received from the RAF during the first Chindit operation, appealed to Col Cochran. As a result, Col Cochran used the circumstance to request 12 B-25H Mitchell medium bombers be diverted from the theater to the 5318th Provisional Unit (Air). Gen Stratemeyer forwarded Col Cochran's request to Arnold and by 21 January, Col Alison had a commitment from Washington (75:6).

Col Cochran got the planes in early February, but he was unable to secure "seasoned" crews. He decided to use fighter pilots to man the aircraft. Given some "green" B-25 crews from the theater, Col Cochran assigned the pilots to other aircraft within the 5318th, primarily the UC-64 of the light-cargo section (65:—). His reasoning was sound. The B-25H model was ideal for close air support as it was equipped with six 50-caliber machine guns and a 75mm cannon. The cannon and the repositioning of the dorsal turret had reduced the crew complement to only five. As configured, the B-25H required only one pilot and could be flown much like a fighter. This convinced Col

Cochran that Maj R. T. (Tadpole) Smith should be the B-25H section commander and Maj Walter V. Radovich should act as Smith's deputy (48:4).

The final section added to the 5318th was the 900th Air Borne Engineers Company. The purpose of this group was to build airfields behind Japanese lines. Complete with air transportable tractors, road graders, and bulldozers, the company mounted an immediate training effort by constructing a completely new landing strip east of Lalaghat. Commanding the 900th Engineers was 1Lt Patrick H. Casey (48:4).

Even before this final piece completed the unit's organizational structure, 5318th personnel were getting a dose of combat. The light planes, gliders, fighters, and bombers were busy gaining experience before the main assault.

During February, the light planes were divided into four sections and dispersed to forward locations in India. The "A" squadron was sent to Ledo to support Gen Wingate's 16th Brigade; "B", to Taro for Gen Stilwell; "C", to Tamu in anticipation of the invasion of Burma; and 10 planes from "D" squadron were temporarily dispatched to support the Arakan front (60:5).

These planes from "D" squadron became embroiled in the Battles of Admin Box. Early in February, the British had become enveloped by a Japanese counter-attack, called Operation HA-GO, and faced complete surrender. Adm Mountbatten ordered the British to hold ground and be resupplied by airdrop. From 4 February until the end of the month, the British fought back and finally defeated the Japanese. During that time, "D" squadron, flying in and out at tree-top level, kept the British spirits high by delivering mail and newspapers, bringing in replacements, and evacuating the wounded. In all, the squadron removed nearly 700 British to a rear airfield for transfer to C-47 Dakotas. Impressed by the light plane pilot's courage and proficiency, Air Marshal Sir John E. A. Baldwin, Commander of the 3rd Tactical Air Force, made a personal visit to offer his congratulations (60:5; 48:7).

Like the light planes, the gliders also flew combat missions during the second month of 1944. On 28 February, a British patrol was loaded aboard a Waco and towed east of the Chindwin River. The glider was cut loose near Minsin. Damaged during landing, the plane was burned and the pilots had to make their

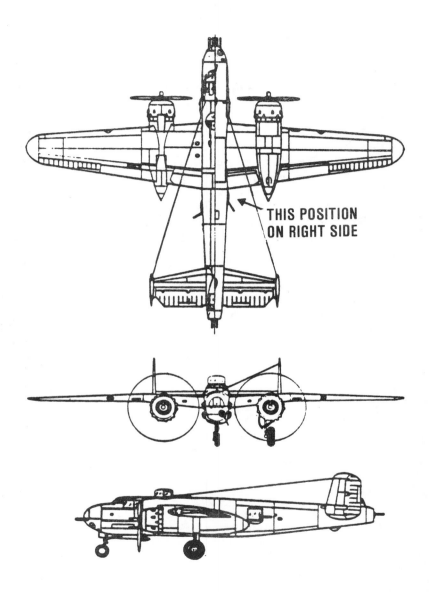

THIS POSITION
ON RIGHT SIDE

Figure 17. B–25H Mitchell.

55

way back to India on foot. The next day, 29 February, gliders were also called on to assist the Chindit's 16th Brigade. Led by Brigadier Bernard E. Fergusson, the brigade had departed Ledo on 1 February and needed assistance in crossing the Chindwin River. Two gliders, carrying folding boats, outboard engines, and gasoline, landed on a sand bar in the Chindwin. After offloading the materiel, they were "snatched" by a C-47 crew and returned to Lalaghat (48:7).

Additionally, starting in February, 5318th crews flew P-51 and B-25 missions into Burma for the first time. On 3 February, Col Cochran led five Mustangs on the unit's first combat mission. The B-25 section joined the fight on 12 February. During the mission, Maj Smith demonstrated the effectiveness of the 75mm cannon to Gen Wingate by blowing the roof off a large building. He later sheepishly admitted he was aiming at a railway switch 200 yards in front of the warehouse (62:March/April 1982:3; 34:21).

From 3 February until 4 March, the 5318th Provisional Unit (Air) flew 54 fighter/bomber missions, concentrating their flights on attacking Japanese lines of communication and increasing their air-to-ground proficiency. From the beginning, fighter and bomber missions concentrated on road and railroad bridges, warehouses, truck convoys, railroad locomotives, and river barges. As the assault section attacked these targets, their accuracy, proficiency, and selection of ordnance improved. Lt Col Smith later described the accuracy attained by his men in the following manner:

Our cannon and [machine guns] were bore-sighted for 1,000 yards, and a typical pass would consist of three cannon rounds at approx[imately] 1,500, 1,000, and 500 yards, interspersed with bursts of [machine gun] fire. This required making allowance for the different ranges by sighting slightly above, then on, and slightly below the target with the optical gun sight. Passes would be initiated at anywhere from 500 to 1,000 feet above ground, and terminated practically on the deck. Most attacks were made at between 200 and 250 mph airspeeds. Now, assuming the air was reasonably calm or only moderately turbulent, most of us could hit a target the size of a one-car garage 50% of the time or better with the 75mm cannon. I know that I, and others in my squadron, scored many direct hits on targets as small as trucks and barracks-type buildings, and accuracy went up accordingly (62:January/February 1982:4).

Equally important as the missions themselves was the intelligence gathered during each sortie. Many of the ranking Chindits flew on the B-25 missions to locate and evaluate jungle clearings for possible use during the invasion. Assisting them was a small detachment, the 10th Combat Camera Unit, using hand-held cameras.

Lacking facilities in which to process film, the commander, 1Lt Charles L. Russhon (Charley Vanilla in Milton Caniff's comic strip (62:April 1981:5)), was forced to improvise. He accomplished his task by developing pictures at night in the open. To keep the area dark, a sentry stood guard on the road leading to the camp. A nearby well furnished the necessary water (48:5).

In addition to the pictures, pilots reported enemy defenses, troop movements, and noted supply lines. This information, when combined with the aerial photographs, would be used by Gen Wingate's staff to plan for his proposed offensive, named Operation THURSDAY.

As Operation THURSDAY neared, the 5318th Provisional Unit was set for action. The organization had mushroomed from a light plane operation into a sizeable assault force. As it grew, the concept of mission support changed also. The use of gliders was a prime example. Originally included for resupply, Col Cochran proposed they be used to air transport one of Gen Wingate's brigades. Later, the idea of building a fortified airstrip was advanced, and the mission of the gliders changed accordingly. By 5 March the training was over, and the 5318th Provisional Unit (Air) was poised to fulfill its part of the Quadrant Conference plan. The next step, the Allied invasion of Burma, would test Gen Arnold's dream. But even up to the scheduled launch, events indicated the execution of Operation THURSDAY was in jeopardy.

Chapter Four

THURSDAY: THE SOLUTION

Throughout the time the 5318th Provisional Unit was training, Southeast Asia Command was developing alternative actions that were not in accord with the Quadrant plan. Adm Mountbatten proposed several operations to the Allied strategic planning staff: BULLFROG, an attack on Akyab Island; CULVERIN, an assault on Sumatra; PIGSTICK, a landing on the Mayu Peninsula; BUCCANEER, an amphibious offensive on the Andaman Islands in the Bay of Bengal; TARZAN, the airborne capture of the Indaw airfield; and finally, AXIOM, a scaled down version of the "dusty" ANAKIM plan (11:Appendix 30). All were either disapproved or abandoned. Brigadier Derek D. C. Tulloch, Gen Wingate's Chief of Staff, became convinced Adm Mountbatten did not want the mission to be conducted (27:175–176).

Col Cochran felt otherwise, but did note some clumsy attempts to misdirect his unit. During the early part of January 1944, Gen Stilwell had attempted to conscript the 5318th Provisional Unit into his camp. After a clarifying letter from Gen Arnold, that idea was scotched, but other CBI units attempted to draw off Col Cochran's resources. Finally, Col Cochran produced a letter from Gen Arnold to Adm Mountbatten with the salutation "Dear Dickie." In the correspondence, Gen Arnold pointedly stated he intended no other use for Col Cochran's unit than to support Gen Wingate. Col Cochran later stated Adm Mountbatten was not at fault; instead, it was the Admiral's staff that was constantly trying to absorb the airplanes, men, and materiel of the 5318th Provisional Unit into existing SEAC organizations (56:188–196).

For whatever reason, under whomever's direction, the net result of these activities was evident. Adm Mountbatten had lost the support of Generalissimo Chiang Kai-shek's Chinese Army, Gen Slim's 14th Corps was not committed to the invasion, and MGen Wingate was irate (27:186). Apart from Gen Wingate's own 16th Brigade, only Gen Stilwell was advancing into Burma. Even Gen Wingate's hand was involved in this assault. Assisting Gen Stilwell were two American LRP units trained by Gen Wingate; established as the 5307th Provisional Unit, they were more commonly known as Merrill's Marauders. Originally intended to augment the Chindits, Gen Wingate had released the Marauders to Gen Stilwell in January (27:164).

By 4 February, Gen Stilwell was marching down the Hukawng Valley when Gen Wingate received orders that indicated his mission had been changed to the following:

(1) To help the advance of Gen Stilwell's combat troops by drawing off and disorganizing the enemy forces opposing them and by preventing the reinforcement of the enemy forces.

(2) To create a favorable situation for Chinese forces to advance Westwards.

(3) To inflict the maximum confusion, damage, and loss on the enemy forces in North Burma (27:168).

As in the first Chindit operation, Gen Wingate was again being sent into Burma without a major offensive or a strategic objective.

First considering resignation, Gen Wingate soon learned through intelligence information the Japanese were massing troops for an invasion of India. He then realized the Japanese would provide the frontal action needed, so he recanted and continued planning Operation THURSDAY (27:169). In doing so, Gen Wingate committed Col Cochran's organization to Operation THURSDAY and to Special Force until the monsoons began.

The plan for the Allied invasion of Burma was straightforward. Under cover of darkness, two small columns of Gen Wingate's Special Force, airborne engineers, and air transportable equipment would be moved by gliders into selected jungle clearings near Katha. Engineers would then prepare landing strips during the day, and transport planes would bring in the remainder of the Chindits on succeeding nights (41:Memorandum for Gen Giles from John R. Alison, 10 April 1944:2). Despite the seeming simplicity, during the planning, preparation, and execution of the plan, adjustments to Operation THURSDAY were constantly required.

Before SEAC published the operating procedures of the mission, the fluid situation around the Indo-Burmese border brought about the first changes. Prior to D-Day, the commandos were scheduled to tow 52 gliders to the area of Tamu to test the plan. The majority of the operation would then be launched from this forward location. Unfortunately, in view of possible Japanese activity in the area, the idea of using Tamu was discarded. Denied the use of this base meant the mission would have to be conducted from Lalaghat, Hailakandi, and Tulihal (Imphal), requiring the Dakotas to climb to 8,000 feet over the Imphal plateau and cross the Chin Hills before heading into Burma (51:2). When the revised plan was finalized, the impact of the additional altitude requirement was not fully recognized.

Gen Wingate released the operating orders for THURSDAY on 29 February. The plan stated on 5 March, C-47 Dakotas would tow 40 gliders each to Broadway (24–45N 96–45E) and Piccadilly (24–29N 96–46E), two jungle clearings named after the major streets of New York City and London. Takeoff time was set for 1700 so the pathfinder gliders would reach the objective areas just after dark. The main force would takeoff 40 minutes later with the interval between takeoffs being one minute apart (48:9).

The units involved were from both British and American organizations. British Brigadier Michael Calvert's 77th Brigade would provide the troops for D-Day; Brigadier W. D. A. Lentaigne's 111th Brigade would be injected into combat three days later. The 3rd West African Brigade, 14th Brigade, and 23rd Brigade would be held in reserve and released as the situation dictated. Seven air force units were to provide aircraft and crews—the 5318th Provisional Unit (USAAF), 315th Troop Carrier Squadron (USAAF), 27th Troop Carrier Squadron (USAAF), 31st Squadron (RAF), 62nd Squadron (RAF), 117th Squadron (RAF), and 194th Squadron (RAF) (50:1).

The 5318th Provisional Unit would spearhead the airborne requirements. Based on the double tow experience of his C-47 crews, Cochran recommended all 26 of his transport pilots be designated aircraft commanders for the mission. With some reluctance, Gen Old agreed to supply the remaining requirement for 13 aircraft and 26 co-pilots. In addition to the Dakotas and Wacos, four days before the mission, UC-64 Norsemen were added to airdrop 1,000 pounds of concertina wire and other material needed to establish strongholds at Piccadilly and Broadway (50:2).

The mission was projected to continue for seven days. The second and third days, 6 and 7 March, were dedicated to airlanding the Chindits at Broadway and Piccadilly airfields. On 8 March, the 111th Brigade would be towed to Chowringhee (23–57N 96–24E), a clearing south of the Shweli River named for Calcutta's major thoroughfare. Duplicating the procedures at Broadway and Piccadilly, the entire operation was to be completed by 11 March (51:9).

A fourth clearing, Templecombe (approximately 23–48N 96–10E), was also to be used, but the procedures varied from the others. Intended for a very small unit, Dah Force, the strip was to be cleared by native Burmese labor under the supervision of a special operations agent (51:7). The date and time of the glider lift to Templecombe was flexible; the mission would be cued by a signal that Templecombe was secured. As events were to prove, the execution of the entire Operation THURSDAY plan was a demonstration in flexibility.

The day of the mission, Air Marshall Baldwin, senior air commander in SEAC, sent the signal that weather conditions were right and Operation THURSDAY was on. Lalaghat was teeming with activity as loud speakers barked out instructions. Tow ropes—each 300 feet long, 11/15 inches in diameter, with enough nylon for 30,000 pair of hose—were stretched out across the ground (67:—). Col Cochran and Gen Wingate would stay behind that night, but many of the others would participate. Col Alison, with a bare minimum of glider flights, would pilot a CG-4A to Piccadilly; Lt Col Olson was headed toward Broadway with the communications gear; and Capt Taylor would fly the lead glider (48:11). Most of the SEAC staff was present. Adm Mountbatten was absent, recovering from an eye injury, but Gen

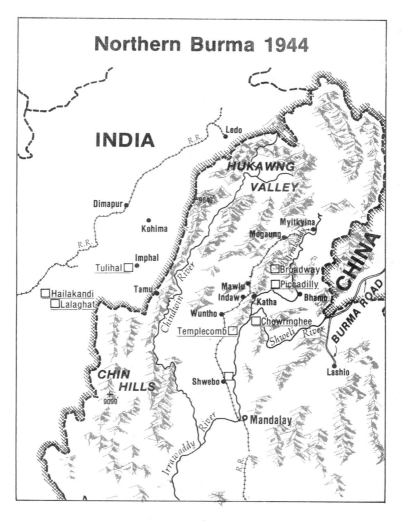

Figure 18. Northern Burma 1944: Operation THURSDAY.

Slim, Air Marshall Baldwin, Gen Stratemeyer, and Gen Old were on hand (47:16).

This entire command structure would be called on when the sudden necessity for change occurred during the execution phase. While Gen Wingate busily directed activities out of a tent at the west end of the runway, Col Cochran, on a hunch, ordered Lt Russhon to take last-minute photographs of the clearings from a B-25 (48:9). Later, nearing scheduled departure time, the solemnity of the operation was brought home when the escape kit was issued—90 silver rupees and a small block of opium (34:21). Col Cochran added to the moment by concluding his mission briefing saying, "Nothing you've ever done, nothing you're ever going to do, counts now. Only the next few hours. Tonight you are going to find your souls." (35:9) Fifteen minutes prior to scheduled takeoff time, a light plane flew into Lalaghat with Lt Russhon aboard. With wet print blow-ups of Piccadilly, Broadway, and Chowringhee, he rushed to show them to Col Cochran and Col Alison. Broadway and Chowringhee were clear, untouched since the last look, but Piccadilly was scattered with logs in a somewhat regular pattern. Two days before, it had been clear. The pattern effectively made Piccadilly a potential death trap for gliders! (21:226–227; 48:9–10) The commanders gathered round the photos to discuss the implications and options.

Two plausible arguments were offered to explain the conditions at Piccadilly. First, the Japanese may have penetrated the plan. If this were true, then Broadway and Chowringhee may have been left open as a trap. The second reason given involved the previous Chindit operation. Piccadilly was the same clearing which British Maj Scott had used in 1943 to air evacuate his men. Since photographs of the area had been published in the 28 June 1943 edition of **Life** magazine, the Japanese did not necessarily have to know about the mission. If they had felled the trees, the Japanese may have done so for precautionary measures. The latter was accepted as most probable (21:226). Hindsight later showed the condition was the result of Burmese teakwood farmers. Regardless of the cause, Piccadilly was ruled out.

The most logical solution was to transfer the Piccadilly troops to Chowringhee; however, it was not the best under the circumstances. Brigadier Calvert opposed this recommendation be-

Figure 19. Piccadilly Conference. (L-R) Russhon, Taylor, Cochran, Alison, Scott, Baldwin, Calvert, Wingate, Tulloch.

cause the Shweli River ran between the two landing zones, thus cutting his brigade in half (51:4). The commanders ruled out cancellation because of the negative effect on morale. Airlifting the entire brigade to one location was the only other option. Gen Slim reduced the requirements to 60 gliders and committed the entire mission to Broadway. Col Cochran took the responsibility for breaking the news to the C-47 and CG-4A crews previously ticketed for Piccadilly. With typical aplomb, Gen Slim wrote, "He sprang on the bonnet to a jeep. 'Say fellers,' he announced, 'we've got a better place to go to!'" (21:228–229) For such a major decision to be made, the British and American commanders delayed the mission only 72 minutes.

As the first C-47 with two gliders in tow lifted off at 1812, the mission was now out of the hands of Gen Wingate and Col Cochran; it belonged to the Dakota crews, the glider pilots, and the forgotten UC-64 section.

For the C-47 aircraft commanders and glider pilots, the climb-out phase was an indication of future problems. Each C-47 pilot was to fly a left-hand box pattern to achieve altitude. The procedure was to hold runway heading for two minutes, turn left for another minute, then left for a base leg of four minutes, left for another minute, and finally left again to fly back over the field. If the Dakota was at or above 2,500 feet while passing over the runway, the pilot continued to Broadway. Some pilots experienced a lower climb rate than anticipated and had to circle over Lalaghat. As this happened, Lt Ulery related, he barely avoided a mid-air collision (69:—).

Unfortunately, additional glider-related problems occurred during the climb to cruise altitude. Four gliders crashed shortly after takeoff; two were cut loose over Lalaghat when their Dakota developed electrical problems; and two more were released over Imphal when their "tug" experienced such high fuel consumption that Broadway was unattainable (50:3). All eight of these gliders landed west of the Chindwin.

For the others, there were problems after crossing the Chin Hills—tow ropes began to fail. Col Cochran later described the difficulties to Gen Arnold:

The moon was almost full but was partially offset by bad haze conditions. Gliders were overloaded, average gross load for each glider being approximately 9,000 lbs. [Technical Data limited gross weight with cargo to

66

Figure 20. Piccadilly.

67

7,500 pounds (67:—)] .... Most of the difficulties were encountered after altitudes of above 8,000 ft. had been reached and mountain ranges and turbulent air had been crossed. As the tow planes started their descent poor visibility over the Chindwin area and the tendency of gliders to overrun the tow plane (accentuated by heavy loads) created a surging of the gliders which was extremely difficult for the pilots. In the worst cases the tow ropes broke. The part in the ropes invariably was caused when both gliders surged at the same time and the shock of the tow rope was taken up simultaneously by the one lead rope (49:8).

A total of nine gliders were lost east of the Chindwin. Lt Col Olson was aboard one of those gliders, as were Maj Richard W. Boebel, intelligence officer; Capt Weldon O. Murphy, a medical officer; and others. The treks back to safety for the downed crews were marked by the heroism of one of the glider mechanics. During a crossing of the Chindwin River, Cpl Estil I. Nienaber, a nonswimmer, was swept away from Maj Boebel's escape party by the strong currents. Rather than call for help and possibly give away the group's position to Japanese patrols, he silently drowned—grimly determined not to utter a sound (25:239; 48:18). Seven of the nine crews eventually made the harrowing journey back to India or on to Broadway (42:5).

By coincidence, the gliders seemed to go down near Japanese headquarters. Two gliders landed in the immediate vicinity of the 31st Divisional Headquarters, two more landed near 15th Divisional Headquarters, and three gliders close to the Regimental Headquarters area. The Japanese interpreted these landings as raiding parties in support of Gen Slim's 4th Corps (51:5). Serendipitously, the tow rope problem had created a diversion. SEAC reported, "It is probable that this diversion assisted for over a week in keeping Japanese attention focussed [sic] away from the area of the main landings . . ." (58:87).

The problems encountered by the gliders at Broadway were not so fortuitous. By 2200, Capt Taylor, in the lead glider, touched down on Broadway and the Chindits fanned out to intercept any Japanese (51:4). There were none. Capt Taylor ordered the green flare lit and positioned the smudge pots. As the succeeding gliders established themselves on the lights, the pilots cut loose at 1,000 feet and began their descent toward Broadway. The extreme overweight conditions caused the glider's approach speed to be much higher than planned.

The resulting landings were unpredictable and hazardous. The second Waco pilot had to crash land his CG-4A to avoid hitting Capt Taylor's glider, while Col Alison, third into the clearing, landed without incident. Col Alison immediately took over command of Broadway. A quick inspection of the ground showed the strip was not as suitable for the assault as photographs had shown. The clearing was traversed with deep ruts from dragged teakwood trees. Tree trunks and water buffalo holes were also masked from aerial photographs by tall elephant grass (14:11). With gliders though, there was no way to turn them back. When they touched down, the speeding gliders caromed off the tree stumps and furrows, ripping off landing gear and smashing to a stop. Without landing gear, the men could not move the crippled gliders out of the path of the incoming waves (61:74). One Waco pilot, 1Lt Donald E. Seese, avoided a disaster by "jumping" his glider over an inert tangle of canvas, steel, and wood (63:—).

To mitigate the congestion, Col Alison and his men rearranged the smudge pots to disperse the landings. The glider assault continued as pairs of gliders plummeted toward the interior of the diamond. For Col Alison, the pace was exhausting; after each pair landed, the pots were repositioned. Most gliders touched down within the landing zone; two did not. They undershot the field and crashed in the jungle, killing all on board; included on one of those gliders was the commander of the engineers, Lt Casey (48:5). Medical Officer, Capt Donald C. Tulloch began treating the wounded during the on-going assault while other personnel tried to extricate trapped men from the twisted wreckage. Complicating Col Alison's problems was an inability to communicate with Col Cochran and Gen Wingate in India; his one radio was damaged during landing (52:10).

Back at Lalaghat, the launch of Dakotas had been followed by a 10-ship formation of UC-64 aircraft. Not adequately equipped for night flying, the wing airplanes soon lost visual contact with lead. Unfortunately, members of the flight had been briefed to simply stay in formation and follow. Capt Wagner and his crew chief, SSgt Felix C. Lockman, Jr., became separated from the others; they continued the mission but were unable to locate the objective area. Returning to India and running low on fuel, they were forced to make an emergency landing at an unknown strip. Luckily it was held by the British. Another UC-64 did not reach

Broadway because the crew had not been properly briefed about the change of landing sites. When they lost sight of the formation, 2Lt Fred H. Van Wagner and Capt Leon R. McMullen flew on to Piccadilly. Seeing no lights, they turned back, not dropping their stores. They too ran short of fuel. Unable to locate Lalaghat because of similar navigation radio frequencies in the area, the two pilots had to bail out (65:—). In total, only two free-fall bundles were dropped near Broadway, and this portion of Operation THURSDAY was considered a failure (48:12).

Meanwhile, the Dakotas had begun returning to Lalaghat slightly later than 2300; after a limited debrief, the crews prepared to fly again. Based on the tow rope difficulties, Gen Old recommended crews no longer pull two gliders. Believing double tow still feasible, Col Cochran launched some Dakotas with two Wacos in trail, but after reconsidering, he agreed to cut back to single tow (50:3). Including those released in the Assam area, a total of 63 gliders were dispatched to Broadway.

Finally, at 0227 on the morning of 6 March, Col Cochran and Gen Wingate received a coded message from Broadway (51:4). Repairs to the damaged radio set had been slow and risky. Periodically dodging the incoming gliders or falling tow lines, Cpl Robert E. True, the communication specialist, worked feverishly to make it operable. Finally able to transmit for a limited time, the single code word, "SOYA-LINK," was sent. Before the mission, Brigadier Tulloch had established only two code words, "PORK-SAUSAGE" and "SOYA-LINK," for the mission. The former would indicate all was well; the latter, named for a meat substitute hated by the British, meant trouble—no more gliders should be dispatched. Due to atmospheric conditions, the message was not received directly from Broadway. Passed through two intermediaries, Col Cochran and Gen Wingate could not know the circumstances at Broadway. Brigadier Tullock wrote, "Those at Lalaghat had a mental picture of parties of men in close contact with an undetermined number of enemy." (51:4–5) They assumed the landing field was under attack!

Wrestling with the situation, Col Cochran ultimately decided to recall the second wave. When the recall was broadcast, all aircraft except one responded. The Dakota that continued had a glider tow of engineering equipment.

An exhausted and discouraged Col Alison was almost asleep

when he heard the last gliders release. To Col Alison's horror, the glider flew beyond the landing field and pranged between two trees. The noise of the crash was deafening; the silence that followed, foreboding. Col Alison was sure everyone on board was dead; however, he was wrong. Auspiciously, the pilot had rigged the bulldozer to the hinged nose of the glider. As the equipment broke its mooring and shot forward, the visor raised the pilots out of the way as the bulldozer cleared. When the nose slammed shut, the only mishap was a broken thumb to the pilot—the equipment was not even damaged. Significantly, on board the last glider was 2Lt Brackett of the airborne engineers, a man who would play an influential role in the completion of Broadway (60:8).

When dawn brought slivers of light to the darkness of the jungle clearing at Broadway, the losses to equipment and personnel became a grim reality. In all, 37 Wacos had arrived; almost all, 34 gliders, were damaged and could not be towed out (51:Appendix E). The injuries to personnel were not as bad as originally thought; only 33 were injured severely enough to require evacuation. Fortunately, the number killed was also low, much lower than Col Alison had anticipated. A total of 31 men were originally reported killed—4 Americans and 27 Chindits (61:76). Later this figure was reduced to a total of 24. The number dead was almost totally comprised of the personnel in the two gliders which crashed into the jungle; only four persons were actually killed on Broadway (51:4). A simple grave was dug in the trees at the edge of the clearing and a Burmese chaplain held a eulogy for the lost comrades in arms.

Balanced against the losses were the accomplishments. During the night, Gen Wingate's staff figured 539 personnel, 3 mules, and 29,972 pounds of stores were delivered to Broadway (48:12). Capt Taylor's report showed a total glider payload of 221,648 pounds on the manifests (49:27). These figures did not include the supplemental supplies added by the Chindits that never appeared on any official documents, nor did it reflect the changes to the loading plan because of Piccadilly. Col Alison later attested to the fact that Gen Wingate's figures were somewhat in error. While he had been frantically directing the glider landings and running from one smudge pot to another, a Chindit had offered him the use of a horse flown in on a Waco glider! (63:—)

Figure 21. CG–4A with visor raised.

Figure 22. Wreckage at Broadway.

73

At 0630 on 6 March, Brigadier Calvert was able to get a message through requesting evacuations planes for the injured. Maj Rebori quickly responded by launching nine L-1 Vigilants, one from Tamu and eight from Taro, and six L-5 Sentinels from Taro. Flying at tree-top level, the light planes arrived over Broadway by early morning. They planned to stay and operate out of this forward base. Rather than expose all the light planes to the enemy, only six patients were actually evacuated that day. The remainder would be airlifted aboard a C-47 when the airfield was finished (61:77).

Alison, seeing the mass of twisted gliders and undulated surface, talked to the surviving engineering officer about preparing the strip. Asked how long it would take to make an airfield, Lt Brackett replied, "If I have it done by this afternoon will that be too late?" (39:4) And he did it! Personnel not needed elsewhere were put on the job. Using manual labor and the undamaged equipment, the men began filling the ruts and flattening the ground. Improvising with teakwood logs between tractors to make crude graders, engineers began to level the field.

Finally, at 1000 Gen Wingate established direct communications with Brigadier Calvert at Broadway. The 77th Brigade commander informed Gen Wingate and Col Cochran the field was secure, they had been unopposed by Japanese, and the airfield should be ready to receive transport planes by nightfall (51:5). Gen Wingate was beside himself with relief and joy! By 1630, the good news was better. A report was forwarded, saying by evening a 4,700-foot strip would be completed and lit (50:3).

The first flight of six Dakotas took off at 1730 with Gen Wingate aboard and Gen Old in the lead airplane. Told to approach from the South, Gen Old chose to land from the North due to traffic. He reported the field was narrow but useable. Troop Carrier Command sent 62 C-47 sorties into Broadway that night, departing from both Lalaghat and Hailakandi (50:3). Col Alison related that Broadway was as busy as any civilian airport, punctuating his remark with "LaGuardia has nothing on us." (2:182). The only accident reported was to two RAF transports; the damage was slight and the planes were flown out two days later.

With the good news about Broadway, Gen Wingate decided to move the 111th Brigade into Chowringhee two days earlier than planned. Based on the previous night's experience, Col

Cochran approved single tow operations and prepared 12 C-47 Dakotas for the job. Like the assault on Broadway, the first gliders contained Chindits and engineers. All made it to destination; however, one Waco overshot the clearing, killing all on board. That glider also contained the only bulldozer slated for Chowringhee (50:3).

Plans for the following day were based on landing transports at Chowringhee the night of 7 March 1944. That day, at about 1200, Lt Col Gaty, commander at Chowringhee, radioed that without the bulldozer, the strip would not be prepared on schedule. Col Cochran immediately dispatched a C-47 to Calcutta to obtain another bulldozer. The load was transferred to a glider which departed for Chowringhee at 2100. At Broadway, Col Alison had also responded by loading one of his bulldozers on a serviceable glider. A C-47 then towed the load to Chowringhee, arriving by 2100. It was still estimated the strip would not be available until after midnight (50:4).

The delayed preparation of Chowringhee required Col Cochran to change plans again, diverting some C-47 sorties to Broadway until Lt Col Gaty was ready. Without Japanese resistance, the landing strip at Broadway had been improved during the day. Based on handling 16 aircraft per hour, Col Cochran ultimately launched 92 C-47 aircraft to Broadway that night. At 2330 the code word "ROORKEE" was received indicating Chowringhee was serviceable for C-47 Dakotas. A 6-ship wave was airborne for Chowringhee by 0029. By the time 24 Dakotas had taken off, Chowringhee reported that only 2,700 feet were lit and approved for use. With 4,500 feet required for night operations, Brigadier Tulloch issued the recall order (51:5–6). Of the seven which did not return, none experienced landing difficulties (50:4).

Even while the airlift into Broadway was being conducted, the men of Col Cochran's assault force were prowling Burma looking for the Japanese Air Force. No Japanese action was observed until 8 March when intelligence discovered the enemy was massing aircraft in the Shwebo area of Central Burma. Deciding to arm each aircraft with a single 500-pound bomb, Lt Col Mahoney led a 21-plane fighter sweep over the enemy airfield at Anisakan, Burma. Discovering about 17 fighters on the ground, Mahoney's formation attacked. After dropping their bombs and auxiliary fuel tanks on anti-aircraft positions, the Mustang pilots set up a strafing pattern, making as many as eight or nine passes (60:10).

On the way back to Hailakandi, Lt Col Mahoney led his flight over the airfields of Onbauk and Shwebo. There the formation found about 60 aircraft—fighters, bombers, transports, and trainers—in the process of landing or already on the ground. Instructed to go for the bombers, the Mustangs duplicated the procedures used in the raid at Anisakan. Diving on the airfields, the assault force continued to make iterative passes until all their ammunition was spent (60:10).

The pilots in the formation had used their bullets wisely. Destroyed on the ground at all the airfields were 27 fighters, 7 bombers, and 1 transport; in the air, the Mustang section added another fighter (52:Appendix D:9). As he departed the area, Lt Col Mahoney alerted the bomber section at Hailakandi to be prepared to launch when the fighters returned (60:10).

Within 45 minutes of landing, Lt Col Smith, who had been flying a P-51, changed planes and flew back to the Onbauk and Shwebo area in a B-25H. Reaching the fields at 2000, the Mitchells pattern-bombed the revetments with fragmentation and incendiary loads, claiming an additional 12 aircraft. When he arrived back at Hailakandi, Lt Col Smith reported the enemy airfields ablaze with buildings, gasoline trucks, and an oil storage depot on fire (52:Annex C).

During the one day, the assault force had destroyed a total of 48 enemy aircraft. One squadron of fighters and 12 bombers accounted for more than 40 percent of all the Japanese aircraft destroyed by the Allies in the CBI during the month of March (60:10; 5:511). Gen Stratemeyer stated, "In one mission [the unit has] obliterated nearly one-fifth of the known Japanese air force in Burma." (60:29 March 1944:8) Intelligence reports also acknowledged the importance of the raid to Operation THURSDAY by observing the mission ". . . no doubt nullif[ied] enemy air opposition to the original fly-in." (53:4)

With this assistance, the operations continued into Chowringhee and Broadway. By 9 March 1944, Gen Wingate decided the location and capacity of Broadway exceeded the value of Chowringhee. Therefore, he sent Brigadier Tulloch to Burma to detail the planned evacuation with the 111th Brigade Commander, Brigadier Lentaigne. The evacuation of Chowringhee was completed by 0600 on the following day—just in time; the Japanese bombed the strip of wrecked gliders at 1300 (51:6). With the emphasis now on Broadway, Gen Wingate poured in men and material. The signal from Templecombe was not received by 11 March, so Gen Wingate transferred Dah Force from Waco gliders to Dakotas and flew them into Broadway (51:7). There was still no Japanese opposition against Broadway when Operation THURSDAY was completed on 11 March.

Figures compiled from various sources indicate the magnitude of THURSDAY. For the entire operation, the following table indicates the amount of men, animals, and equipment airlifted.

TABLE 1 Operation THURSDAY Summary

Location	Personnel	Horses	Mules	Weight of Stores
Broadway	7,023	132	994	444,218 pounds
Chowringhee	2,029	43	289	64,865 pounds
Grand Total	9,052	175	1,283	509,083 pounds

Of these figures, the 5318th Provisional Unit (Air) was responsible for 2,038 personnel, 16 horses, 136 mules, and 104,681 pounds of stores. Including the glider dispatched from Broadway, a total of 80 gliders were launched—63 to Broadway and 17 to Chowringhee. Personnel sent to the two strips by glider totalled 971. The C-47 effort, which included Troop Carrier Command and RAF flights, amounted to 579 sorties (48:14; 49:Annex 3; 50:4).

Although these are impressive figures, the most momentous feature of the operation was the establishment of an airfield and the delivery of fresh troops more than 200 miles behind enemy lines. By landing soldiers beyond those lines, the Allies, for the first time, used airpower for the backbone of an invasion. As soon as the Chindits landed, they formed columns and disappeared into the shadowed jungles. Their purpose was to strangle the supply lines of the Japanese by controlling choke points. As they stalked their way across the jungle floor, the 3rd Indian Division would continue to call on Col Cochran's men to be their artillery armada for close air support, their umbilical cord for supplies, and their airborne ambulances for the evacuation of casualties.

Chapter Five

AIRPOWER: THE APPLICATION

As elements of the 3rd Indian Division arrived at Broadway during Operation THURSDAY, they formed into columns and set out into separate areas of Northern Burma. Brigadier Calvert's 77th Brigade drove west toward the railroad line between Mandalay and the enemy airfield at Myitkyina. Near Mawlu, the brigade was to establish a roadblock and keep supplies from reaching Gen Stilwell's opposition in the Hukawng Valley, the Japanese 18th Division. Brigadier Lentaigne's 111th Brigade was to push west-southwest toward Wuntho to cut off Japanese replacements going north by rail and road (4:26–27). Brigadier Fergusson's Brigade, exhausted from the trek across the Chin Hills, was expected to capture the Nippon supply hub of Indaw before the monsoons. There, Gen Wingate hoped to use the two all-weather enemy airfields of Indaw East and Indaw West (11:218; 27:213–218). A fourth LRP unit was also injected into Burma; Gen Wingate committed his reserve 3rd West African Brigade to Broadway for garrison support (2:110–111).

Col Cochran and Gen Wingate agreed to retain Broadway as a supply site and a harbor for the light planes. Norsemen and Dakotas kept the flow of supplies going into the heartland of Burma at night through this airfield. Approximately 30 light planes operated daily out of this behind-the-line bastion, and the strip also served the 1st Air Commando Group (officially as of 29 March 1944) as an emergency airfield (48:15; 60:9). Strategically, Broadway was invaluable.

On 13 March, two days after the completion of Operation THURSDAY, Japanese fighters finally found Broadway and tried to dislodge the air commandos. Gen Wingate had anticipated the problem by positioning RAF Spitfires, as well as P-51A Mustangs, on the field, but the fighters proved too vulnerable to enemy attacks. The air attacks occurred almost daily; personnel casualties were low but radio equipment, an early warning radar set, and a few light planes were damaged (48:15). Nevertheless, the jungle citadel remained firmly in the hands of the Allies. Later, Japanese ground forces engaged Col Claude Rome and his Chindit garrison troops; however, they were repulsed. Like frustrated children, the Japanese slashed at the canvas skin of the light planes with bayonets before receding into the jungle (68:—). The airfield was never overrun and was protected enough to eventually include maintenance shops, a hospital, a small garden, and even a chicken farm! (16:115)

Meanwhile, the Chindits were being supplied by Troop Carrier Command. Constantly reconnoitering the area for possible drop zones, the brigades literally lived and functioned from one drop to another. When Gen Wingate's troops passed a message to India that a clearing was available, C-47 Dakotas would be scheduled to takeoff after dark and fly to the coordinates given. As they neared the site, the Dakota pilots searched for an L-shaped row of lights to pinpoint the Chindit position (12:167). This was always a critical time because of the exposure of the C-47 and Special Force.

At first, all drops were made using parachutes, but results were spotty. The Chindits reported loads landing anywhere near the zone to some distance away because of winds. Finally, to lessen the drift effect, only delicate loads were rigged with chutes; the remainder were pushed out the door to free fall to the awaiting troops below (12:168). The supplies contained anything and everything consumable for the brigades—food, ammunition, and medicine. Special Force would then gather the stores and disappear into the undergrowth.

Although the supply drops were normally conducted at night, the light plane functions required actions during broad daylight. Precautionary measures were necessary. If the Chindits had injuries, casualties, or jungle sicknesses, they requested evacuation support, provided the location of a suitable clearing, and established an arrival time. To locate the ever-moving brigades, the light plane pilots (commonly called L-pilots) instituted a signal system to assure positive identification. Codes were tried and soon abandoned except when used in conjunction with map co-ordinates and time over target; decoding caused response time to be too slow and required centralized control. In short order, satisfactory results were attained by using aerial mosaic photographs and setting aside one frequency, 4530 kHz, for all ground-to-air radio traffic (52:11). Combining the mosaics and direct communication, a Chindit RAF liaison officer could describe ground locations from the perspective of the pilot flying overhead. As a final precaution, before attempting to land or drop supplies, the L-pilots also looked for predetermined visual signals such as "Very" flares, smoke, or panels (52:9).

Unlike the debilitating effect on the 1943 LRP expedition, treatment of casualties by this time became a source of high morale. Under normal circumstances, the wounded were brought back to Broadway and transferred to a UC-64 Norseman or a C-47 Dakota. When a soldier required immediate attention, the L-pilots would fly directly to hospitals in India if possible. Also, the air commando UC-64 pilots augmented the L-series planes by flying to larger clearings to evacuate up to 10 litter patients at a time (65:—). Even though the L-1 was supposed to only carry a maximum of three patients, Chindits reported it was not uncommon to see a Vigilant stagger skyward with five to seven casualties on board (68:—). Col Alison later gave a testimonial to the effectiveness of the commando air evacuation effort by saying, "A man could be wounded anywhere in the battle area and that night he would be in a hospital in India." (38:9)

It was not long before the air commandos recognized the versatility of the L-5 Sentinel; they expanded the role accordingly. Husbanding the L-1 Vigilants for air evacuation, the light plane section found a number of uses for the ubiquitous L-5. Often these aircraft were the vital backup supply link to the stealthy Chindits. Rigging 75-pound parachute packs to the bomb racks, the Sentinels made emergency airdrops of ammunition or food to brigades who had been missed during normal C-47 resupply missions. In addition to dropping supplies, the pilots used their imagination to develop new applications for the light planes. The following are examples of functions ultimately performed by Sentinels in support of Special Force:

(1) Transporting headquarters personnel,
(2) Dropping medical supplies,
(3) Landing replacements,
(4) Evacuating prisoners of war,
(5) Transporting glider personnel,
(6) Making reconnaissance flights,
(7) Returning captured documents and material,
(8) Transporting official orders,
(9) Delivering mail,
(10) Gathering intelligence information, and
(11) Spotting targets for the assault sections (59: Report of Air Marshall Baldwin on Operation THURSDAY:5).

Never before used on this scale or in this fashion, the light planes performed spectacularly (53:6). Early in the operation, Gen Wingate expressed his appreciation of the L-pilots by saying, "Without you men and your aircraft, this campaign could not have hoped to be a success." (54:5)

Bouyed by the actions of the air commandos, Gen Wingate felt confident about his air power theory. By the third week of March, the Chindits were crouched in four locations preparing to leap on the logistic tail of the Japanese dragon. While waiting for Special Force to deploy, the P-51A Mustangs and B-25H Mitchells had roamed the skies of Northern Burma striking supply lines, roads, bridges, airfields, and more. When Brigadier Calvert radioed that his brigade was entrenched on a hill overlooking the railroad line outside Mawlu, the assault force refocused its attention on close air support.

Although a semi-permanent stronghold defied the LRP principle of speed and mobility, the addition of airpower made it possible. Brigadier Calvert installed his roadblock on 17 March and immediately began using the 1st Air Commando Group to dig in. The following day, although they were unable to establish radio contact, the air assault force dove on enemy positions marked by smoke and dropped depth charges and fragmentation bombs. As a result, the Japanese remained quiet for three days and then rushed the stronghold under a volley of mortar fire and machine guns; the attack was turned back. Using anti-tank guns and ammunition supplied by gliders, Calvert's men had fortified the position, established the perimeter with concertina wire, and

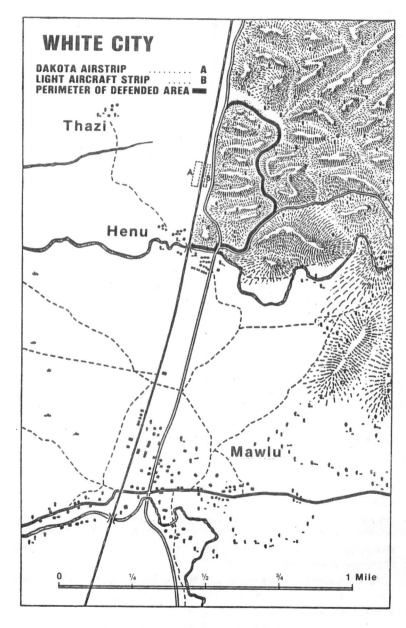

Figure 23. White City Stronghold.

hunkered down for a long siege. To keep the Chindit blocking action continually supplied, consumables had to be airdropped into the citadel on a daily basis. The stronghold soon took on the name White City because of the plethora of parachutes hanging from the trees. The roadblock withstood the repeated attacks and caused a serious supply and munition problem for the Japanese 18th Division (55:60).

Just five days after Calvert had begun setting up his stronghold of White City, the 16th Brigade was in position to begin an attack on Indaw. Because of the long march from Ledo, Gen Wingate decided to commit the 14th Brigade to assist Brigadier Fergusson's weary men. Therefore, on 22 March, Gen Wingate signaled the 1st Air Commando Group to begin construction of another airstrip northwest of Indaw. Using the same techniques as Broadway, C-47 Dakotas towed six gliders with construction equipment to level the new strip, christened Aberdeen (52:7).

While Aberdeen was being built, the enemy fought fiercely to keep the Chindits from severing the key supply line through Indaw. One of Gen Wingate's columns was pinned down during the fighting and requested a napalm strike to assist their retreat. The P-51A Mustangs responded by making shallow dive-bombing and strafing attacks while Special Force ground troops directed the action. The fighter pilots had to conserve their ammunition, so they interspersed numerous dummy runs with live approaches. Special Force and the air commandos achieved a high degree of coordination by marking the enemy positions with mortar smoke and friendly positions with "Very" flares. Able to separate themselves from the Japanese, the Chindits ultimately worked their way back to safety (2:147).

The withdrawal was a success but casualties were high. By the end of the first week of the operation, over 150 light plane missions had been flown, over 200 casualties had been evacuated, and almost 75 supply drops had been accomplished in support of Aberdeen (52:8). The enemy desperately needed Indaw because the supply hub now played a major role in the Nippon strategic plans for the conquest of India (4:289).

As the Chindits were being flown into Burma during Operation THURSDAY, Lt Gen Renya Mutaguchi, commander of the Japanese 15th Army, launched his own invasion. It was a 3-pronged attack into India called Operation U-GO. The Japanese 33rd

Figure 24. Northern Burma 1944: March–May.

85

Division advanced from south of Tamu; the 15th Division, from east of Imphal; and the 31st Division, through the Tuza Gap east of Kohima. The Japanese 18th Division in the Hukawng Valley was also involved; they were to block Gen Stilwell's Chinese troops from joining in the fight (55:48-49). The genesis of the plan could be traced to Operation LONGCLOTH. As a result of Gen Wingate's first expedition, Gen Mutaguchi had determined the Japanese defensive posture in Burma was vulnerable (55:7). Therefore, he decided to cut off the British from their supply depot at Imphal and interpose Japanese troops on Indian soil prior to the monsoons. From this "toehold," he would increase his outer perimeter of defense. Additionally, Gen Mutaguchi planned to use the operation to generate favorable propaganda for a "March to Delhi" by Indian National Army leader Chadra Bose (11:446). Gen Mutaguchi hoped the U-GO offensive would be swift, lasting less than a month, as the invading troops were provided only a 21-day ration of supplies (55:41). Each division would provide its own provisions along the avenue of advance until the invasion; thereafter, the Japanese would move stores by the Shwebo-Imphal Road as well as the previous supply routes (55:49). The only all-weather artery was between Shwebo and Imphal; inauspiciously, the "dry season only" routes were near the area of Gen Wingate's Chindits.

With the required major offensive now in being and knowing the poor supply conditions of the Japanese, Gen Wingate felt he was on the verge of proving LRP theory. He immediately dispatched an optimistic letter to Winston Churchill concerning the situation (27:223). Tragically, within days of reading the news, the Prime Minister was shocked to learn the circumstances in Burma had changed.

For Special Force, lightning struck on 24 March and the direction of the wind forever shifted against the Chindits. Gen Wingate flew to the front lines in a L-5 on 23 March to observe the operations and discuss strategy with his brigade commanders (11:212). After the conferences, he proceeded to Broadway where he boarded an air commando B-25H (52:2). Following an intermediate stop at Imphal, the aircraft headed west for Gen Wingate's headquarters at Shylet. It never arrived. On the last leg of his journey, the Mitchell bomber inexplicably exploded into the side of a hill, killing all on board.

Mystery and intrigue accompanied the crash. Strangely, despite the flight path, the aircraft impacted sharply into the west side of the mountain range—it was heading east! (68:—) Questions were raised about engine trouble, weather, and even sabotage; none of the answers were conclusive. The aircraft nosed-in and the wreckage was severely confined. The only recognizable clue to the passengers on board was located near the crash site; it was the familiar pith helmet of the Chindit commander (68:—). Those who died along with Gen Wingate were Capt T. G. Borrow, his adjutant; Stewart Emeny and Stanley Wills, war correspondents; 1Lt Brian F. Hodges, pilot; 2Lt Stephen A. Wanderer, navigator; TSgt Frank Sadoski, SSgt James W. Hickey, and SSgt Vernon A. McIninch, crewmembers (27:286). Interestingly, according to the rules of war, all the bodies, including that of Gen Wingate were buried at Arlington Cemetery outside Washington DC.

Gen Wingate's death came in the midst of the most complicated operation ever attempted in that theater and robbed the Allies of a colorful and dynamic commander (52:2–3). In selecting a successor, Gen Slim did not choose an original Chindit, such as Brigadier Calvert or Brigadier Fergusson. Neither did Slim pick Gen Wingate's Chief of Staff, Brigadier Tulloch; instead, he opted for the most orthodox officer within Gen Wingate's former command—Brigadier Lentaigne. The new Special Force commander's credentials were beyond reproach; he was a competent and heroic officer. However, he did not endorse LRP theory, nor was he favorably impressed with the late Gen Wingate (2:161). Although Col Cochran's mission would not change, events soon showed that under Gen Lentaigne, the ideals of LRP were discarded. By mid-April the Chindits would begin to form large formations and attack fortified positions. For the time being though, the operations continued with the air commandos giving direct ground support to columns at the stronghold at White City, at the C-47 airfield of Aberdeen, along the supply roads and bridges west of Wuntho, and to a splinter unit from the 77th Brigade cutting the traffic lines between Lashio and Myitkyina.

All the air commando sections helped the Chindits, not always in the most conventional way possible. The Japanese communication system proved particularly vulnerable to one of the air commandos' maverick schemes. The tactic required an unapproved modification to the fighters. Laying a 450-foot cable around the rear of a Mustang, ordnance specialists connected the ends to each of the wing bomb racks. Attached to this cable was a weight which made the device drag behind during takeoff; once airborne, it hung like a pendulum beneath the cruising P-51. The assault force pilots would use the cable assembly to cut Japanese communications by diving on telephone and telegraph lines, pulling up just in time to wrap the weight around the wires like a bola. Normally, the lines snapped, but occasionally, pilots reported uprooting telephones poles and dragging them for miles before jettisoning the cable! One overzealous pilot even resorted to using his plane like a flying wire cutter after losing his cable assembly—slicing through several telephone lines before heading back to Hailakandi. (48:17; 66:—)

But the assault force was not the only offensive arm of the air commandos. Toward the end of the first month of the invasion, a frustrated transport crew supplemented its airland resupply missions by trying a hand at bombardment. On 25 March, while making a supply run into Broadway, a Dakota pilot dropped two mortar shells on some Japanese trucks. Three days later, the same crew spotted another convoy of mechanized transport and dropped fragmentation bombs, mortars, and incendiary bombs from the side door of the C-47. The pilot explained, "We may not have done any damage but I'll bet we scared the hell out of them." (60:12)

March closed with two important personnel changes. During the month, command of the L-1/L-5 section changed hands. The need for the change came to light when one of the squadrons moved up to an airfield called Dixie, inside the border of Burma. Shortly after flying operations had begun, intelligence reports indicated the enemy was advancing in the area and would soon overrun the strip. Acting on short notice, the hasty departure from Dixie was not accomplished well. Code books and reports were left behind. More seriously, Staff Sergeant Raymond J. Ruksas, another deployed L-pilot was not informed the field had been abandoned. When he returned, luckily the enemy had not penetrated the camp (68:—). In the aftermath of the debacle, Col Cochran decided to alter the organization of the light plane section because the operations of four separate squadrons could not be tracked adequately. As a result of the change, the L-series aircraft were placed under the command of Lt Col Gaty (52:8).

The other personnel move left Col Cochran without his right hand man. On 28 March, Gen Arnold called Col Alison home to help establish more air commando units. At Broadway when summoned, Alison wasted no time getting back to India. Commandeering a RAF Dakota with a badly damaged wing, Alison flew the crippled plane out. Because he had never flown the C-47 before, he requested help from a pilot in the tower at Hailakandi before landing. (63:—). By the time he touched down, Col Alison had a second message requesting he brief Gen Dwight D. Eisenhower's European Theater Staff on Operation THURSDAY. He departed India on 1 April for Washington by way of the British Isles (52:2).

Under the dual leadership of Cols Cochran and Alison, the air commandos had accumulated an impressive set of statistics. The C-47 Dakotas had flown in over 450,000 pounds of supplies during March, and the CG-4A Waco gliders had delivered an additional 310,000 pounds. The light planes estimated they evacuated 1,200 to 1,500 casualties before the end of the first month of the operation (52:6–8). Damage inflicted by the assault force during March is shown in Table 2.

TABLE 2
Assault Force Damage Report for March

Category	Destroyed
Aircraft	50
Trucks	29
Rolling Stock	48
Locomotives	4
Bridges	8
Warehouses	38
Bashas	55
Ammunition Sites	7 (60:12)

During this critical month of action, the Allies established air superiority over Burma for the first time. USAAF records indicate the Japanese lost 117 airplanes in the third month of 1944

(5:511). Significantly, the 1st Air Commando Group—only a single squadron of fighters and 12 bombers—accounted for 42.7 percent of the total Japanese aircraft destroyed! And the following month would be equally impressive.

Early in April, the air commandos "reprised" the Anisakan-Onbauk-Shwebo mission; only the location changed. Acting on intelligence information of Japanese movement in the area of Rangoon, the commando assault force took off at 0800 on 4 April heading for Aungban, Burma. Just prior to the arrival of the Mustangs, the Japanese had scrambled their fighters from Heho to parry a P-38 attack from the USAAF 459th Squadron. Shortly after the enemy fighters recovered into Aungban, Lt Col Mahoney's P-51A Mustangs arrived over the airfield. Finding the Japanese aircraft parked next to and in revetments, the commandos kept the anti-aircraft batteries at bay with rockets while strafing the field on continual passes. The assault force destroyed 4 medium bombers and 20 fighters on the ground. In the air, Capt Forcey dove on an enemy aircraft, making a pass within 200 yards before pulling off; the Japanese fighter poured smoke and exploded. On the way home, the fighters also destroyed an enemy bomber on the ground at Anisakan. The total enemy losses were 26 verified kills, and the air commandos did not lose any P-51A Mustangs during the mission (52:Annex C).

As the Allies asserted air superiority over Burma, the work of the air commandos showed dramatic results. The situation at White City illustrated this aspect. The Japanese had continued their pressure on White City, storming Calvert's position almost daily since the block had been established. Likewise, the fighters and bombers of assault force frequently pounded the Japanese positions around the stronghold (11:283–286). Throughout this time, the light planes removed casualties from a small strip constructed next to the railroad line. Because there was no enemy air opposition, a L-5 Sentinel pilot offered to fly Brigadier Calvert over the surrounding area to locate and record enemy concentrations (2:200).

To dislodge the Japanese, Calvert used this new information to request bombing attacks within 50 yards of his own position. The accuracy of the air commando attacks and the incessant bombing finally proved too much for the Imperial troops. On 15 April, a Chindit wrote in his diary, ". . . air action on this occasion against the enemy has been consistent and destructive. Amongst other things it has been shown that aircraft alone can force the enemy to move or leave his artillery." (53:Appendix B:1) The air attacks had caused the Japanese to break ranks and run, leaving behind everything—dead, documents, equipment, and weapons! (2:126) With this kind of help from Col Cochran's men, Special Force effectively blocked the rail line into Myitkyina for nearly two months. As a result, the holding action by the Japanese 18th Division was impossible (20:223).

Meanwhile at Aberdeen, 16th Brigade continued to use the 1st Air Commando Group and Troop Carrier Command to resupply their attempt to secure Indaw. On the night of 7 April, a Nippon fighter pilot sent a shudder through the transport organizations when he intercepted a RAF Dakota on approach at Aberdeen. The C-47 suffered damage to the landing gear and lost one engine, but the pilot was able to land without casualties (52:7). Nevertheless, the effect of this incident was profound. The Allies could no longer assume flights into behind-the-line airfields would be conducted with impunity. Thereafter, C-47 Dakota sorties were synchronized to arrive and depart stronghold airstrips at dusk and dawn. Additionally, fighter escorts were assigned to patrol the area. Fortunately, the attack was not repeated and all future transport flights were conducted without incident (52:7).

The attack at Aberdeen did not affect the L-pilots though; they continued flying unescorted while establishing a reputation for courage and skill. In supporting the Chindits, the air commandos were known for their ability to fly out of places others could not. For example, when Merrill's Marauders were pinned down at Nhpum Ga, their own L-4 Grasshoppers were unable to extricate the sick and wounded because of the small landing strip. Gen Stilwell immediately ordered the air commando L-1 Vigilants to air evacuate the casualties. Altogether, the light planes took out over 350 hospital cases (68:—).

The light plane pilots further enhanced their reputation by developing a novel method of air support that proved to be very effective. During the construction of Aberdeen, one of Brigadier Fergusson's RAF liaison officers became separated from his column and discovered a large supply dump in the jungle around Indaw (4:289). When he finally returned to his brigade, the officer requested assistance from the air commandos.

Frustrated because he was unable to establish the location of the site using maps or aerial mosaics, Lt Col Gaty asked the RAF officer to fly with him in a L-5 Sentinel to reconnoiter the area. Pinpointing the position, he returned to Aberdeen to set up a rendezvous with the assault force. As the P-51A Mustangs and B-25H Mitchells arrived at a pre-arranged point, Lt Col Gaty had the RAF liaison officer mark the target with a smoke bomb as the L-5 cleared the tree tops. The Mustangs and Mitchells delivered their ordnance on the smoke (48:20–21). Due to the success of this coordinated mission, the light plane pilots continued to use "forward air controller" methods and occasionally even dropped grenades on small targets themselves (65:—).

In support of all the Chindit brigades, Col Cochran's men were also employed in a more orthodox role. Targeted against Japanese surface and river lines of communication, the air commandos were equally effective. Flying replacement P-51B Mustangs, the assault force attacked the Shweli River bridge, a target which had on numerous occasions withstood Eastern Air Command bomber attacks. The bridge controlled a major supply route to Northern Burma. On 21 April, Maj Petit proved the accuracy of the dive-bombing Mustangs when he scored a direct hit with two 1,000-pound bombs and collapsed the span (60:13). This is only one example. By the end of the campaign, the road and railroad system of Burma was so confused, the Japanese were unable to move supplies from Northern Burma to their only useable traffic artery—the Shwebo-Imphal road (55:62).

While the assault force hammered on the Japanese lines of communication, the light plane force concentrated on the evacuation of casualties. In April, the 1st Air Commando Group made military history by placing the YR-4 helicopter into combat. Unfortunately, the helicopters Col Alison had worked so hard to secure proved to be less useful than hoped. Of the original four rotary-winged aircraft, two were lost before they had flown a successful mission in the CBI. Enroute to India, a C-46 transport crashed while carrying one of the untested craft. A helicopter pilot flew a second one into a power line on a training mission and crashed, killing a passenger. Finally, on 21 April, 1Lt Carter Harman flew a YR-4 on a rescue mission into Burma to evacuate a light plane pilot forced down on a Japanese-controlled road. The downed L-pilot and his passengers were directed to seek shelter in the hills while awaiting the rescue. Because of overheating problems, the helicopter flew by stages to Aberdeen. When he arrived on 23 April, Lt Harman was immediately pressed into action. He successfully transferred the pilot and three casualties to awaiting L-1 Vigilants and returned to Aberdeen on 24 April. Lt Harman continued to fly combat missions until 4 May. When Aberdeen came under heavy Japanese bombardment, Lt Col Gaty ordered Lt Harman and his craft back to India. In the 23 combat sorties performed, the concept of the helicopter was proved; however, the YR-4 was grossly underpowered and eventually was withdrawn after the engine failed due to overheat (52:12).

The month of April again provided some impressive statistics for the 1st Air Commando Group. Table 3 shows the damage inflicted by the assault force during April.

TABLE 3
Assault Force Damage Report for April

Category	Destroyed
Aircraft	35
Trucks	4
Rolling Stock	6
Bridges	3
Barracks	45
Bashas	130
Ammunition Sites	5
Anti-aircraft Positions	11 (60:14-15)

United States Army Air Force records indicate during the month of April the Japanese lost 107 planes (5:511). For the second month in a row, the contribution of the 1st Air Commando Group was staggering; the Mustangs and Mitchells accounted for 32.7 percent of the total Japanese aircraft destroyed within the CBI Theater.

May marked the sixth month that the air commandos had been in India. According to Gen Arnold's plan, on 1 May Col Cochran's men were scheduled to be relieved of duty and sent back to the US. The plan was altered because, as Col Cochran said,

". . . we kept wanting to protect those troops that were still in there." (56:288) As of 17 May, the 3rd Indian Division officially came under operational control of Gen Stilwell, but even prior to that time he had ordered the 111th, 14th, and 3rd West African Brigades to move north toward Mogaung (20:221). Gen Stilwell wanted the three brigades to link up with Brigadier Calvert's men to assault the Japanese garrison located there.

The 16th Brigade had already been sent back to India in early May. In Burma longer than the other units, Brigadier Fergusson's men showed signs of sickness, exhaustion, and strain (58:91). Gen Slim ordered their withdrawal. The other four brigades were in equally bad shape, but Gen Stilwell would not allow them to be relieved. He feared their retreat would attract Japanese troops toward his position (20:221). After "salting" Broadway, Aberdeen, and White City with land mines, the Chindits abandoned their strongholds and began working their way north through the jungles and rice paddies.

The 111th Brigade, now commanded by Col John Masters, was responsible for applying further pressure on the logistic lines that fed the Japanese 18th Division. On 9 May, Col Masters selected a site and requested gliders to build an airstrip. Known as Clydeside, the block was redesignated Blackpool when the original name was compromised (53:3). Despite valiant fighting, the 111th Brigade never fully secured the stronghold, in part because Gen Mutaguchi released some of his U-GO reserve soldiers to fight the Chindits (55:61). The full brunt of these fresh troops flushed Special Force out of Blackpool after only two weeks. Another part of the problem at Blackpool was weather—the monsoons broke before the brigade could get entrenched (12:213). Flying during the intervals between squall lines, the assault force shelled and bombarded the perimeter of the bastion, but the support lacked continuity.

Just before the monsoons, the air force of the Rising Sun made a last ditch attempt to regain control over Burma by bringing up large numbers of replacements (5:511). It was too little, and it was too late. On 19 May, the fighter section had just arrived at Blackpool when a flight of 16 Nippon warplanes was spotted. Salvoing their bombs on Japanese positions around the stronghold, the air commandos attacked the enemy fighters and bombers. During the dogfight, the P-51 pilots shot down one bomber and two fighters. There was no damage to the seven Mustangs (53:Annex C:2).

This was the air commandos' last hurrah; weather was now critically hampering the effectiveness of the group. Col Cochran tried to operate out of the airfields in Eastern India as long as possible; it was a dangerous gamble. The rains soaked the grass strips at Hailakandi and Lalaghat, turning them into quadmires. At one point, Col Cochran felt he had waited too long. He related, "We had one tough rain where actually there was a couple of feet of water on the landing strip." (56:288) Unable to avoid the pending torrent, Col Cochran ordered the air commandos back to Asansol, an abandoned British airfield in Central India. On 23 May, the last UC-64 raised a "rooster tail" as it slogged down Halakandi's grass strip for the final time. The pilot's log read, "Beat bad storm by inches." (65:—)

Once the air commandos arrived in Asansol, the number of personnel began to thin out. Col Cochran convinced Gen Stilwell to send men back to the US if they had completed two tours of duty in the war (56:290). Falling into that category was Col Cochran himself. Before departing for Washington and eventually Gen Eisenhower's staff, he relinquished the 1st Air Commando Group to Col Gaty. In turn, Lt Col Boebel took over the far-flung light plane section (53:2).

Lt Col Boebel ordered all the light planes back to India; however, he was unaware part of his section stayed in Burma to fly casualties to hospitals. Without the strength of their air artillery, the 111th Brigade had retreated from Blackpool on 24 May and fled westward toward Lake Indawgyi. Col Masters described the support he received during the withdrawal as follows: "The American pilots of the Light Plane Force came, hour after hour, day after day, to the little patch of swamp we had made into a strip, and shuttled back through the heaving skies." (12:234) A group of eight light plane pilots continued evacuating Col Masters' sick and wounded until an alternative solution was found (35:17). Finally, Col Masters convinced Gen Lentaigne to divert a Sunderland seaplane from the Bay of Bengal to Lake Indawgyi to assist the effort (12:233). Altogether, nearly 400 casualties were airlifted to hospitals northeast of Dimapur (58:91). When Lt Col Boebel located the group, the light plane commander immediately ordered them to return to India. This was the final action of the 1st Air Commando Group during the 1943–44 dry season.

The effect of the air commandos' protection and support of the 3rd Indian Division was felt as far away as Imphal and Kohima. After an initial success and savage fighting, the Japanese U-GO offensive was pushed back. As the Imperial troops fled toward their previous sanctuary of Burma, Gen Slim pursued with a vengence. After the war, the Imperial Army generals spoke of the failed offensive and pointed out very succinctly their assessment of the impact of Operation THURSDAY and the LRP phase that followed: "The penetration of the airborne force into Northern Burma caused the failure of the Army plan to complete the Imphal Operations . . . the airborne raiding force . . . eventually became one of the reasons for the total abandonment of Northern Burma." (55:61) In a monograph, Gen Mutaguchi and others stated specifically, the operation had the following impacts:

(1) The [15th] Army was unable to advance its headquarters until the end of April because it was forced to provide measures against the airborne force. Consequently, communication with various groups became inadequate and eventually caused a hostile attitude between the Army and its divisions in later operations.

(2) Transportation of supplies to units engaged in the Imphal Operations became very difficult because of damage to roads which prevented the transfer of vehicles from the rear preparation area to the Shwebo-[Imphal] Road.

(3) Elements of the 15th Division, 24th Independent Mixed Brigade, and 53rd Division scheduled for the Imphal operation, were involved elsewhere.

(4) The 5th Air Division was forced to operate against the enemy airborne unit.

(5) The 18th Division which was fighting desperately in the Hukawng area had to deal with an increasingly difficult situation due to interception of the supply route (55:62).

Furthermore, Lt Gen T. Numata, Chief of Staff of the Japanese Southern Army, affirmed the impact by saying, "The difficulty encountered in dealing with the airborne forces was ever a source of worry to all the headquarters staffs of the Japanese army and contributed materially to the Japanese failure in the Imphal and Hukawng operations." Apparent from the remarks of Lt Gen E. Naka, Chief of Staff, Japanese Burma Area Army, is the effectiveness of the air commando's "forward air controller" raids on the supply dumps at Indaw. He certified the Indaw lines of communication became useless as they were "wiped out by bombing and ground raids." (4:289)

Because actions speak louder than words, the most telling argument for the operation can be found in Lt Gen K. Sato's actions during Operation U-GO. By late April, his unit, the 31st Division, was feeling the effects of THURSDAY; they were very short of ammunition, provisions, and food. In May, Gen Sato sent a message to Gen Mutaguchi stating, "Since leaving the Chindwin we have not received one bullet from you, nor a grain of rice." (23:230) Food was in such short supply, some men subsisted on grass and black slugs; sickness, such as beriberi, was sapping the 31st Division's fighting ability (55:73). Finally, Gen Sato radioed Gen Mutaguchi that he was withdrawing from Kohima. When threatened with a court martial, Gen Sato replied, "Do what you please. I will bring you [Gen Mutaguchi] down with me." (23:230) Ordered back into the fray, he refused again saying, "The 15th Army has failed to send me supplies and ammunition since the operation began. This failure releases me from any obligation to obey the order—and in any case it would be impossible to comply." (16:156)

Clearly, from the testimony, the first air invasion in military history was instrumental in defeating the Imperial Japanese Army. Additionally, Gen Wingate's LRP theory was completely substantiated. The air commandos and the Chindits had caused widespread confusion and uncertainty behind the enemy's forward areas which led to a progressive weakening and misdirection of the Japanese main forces. Heavily influenced by the actions of the 1st Air Commando Group and the 3rd Indian Division, a nation known for fanatical obedience suffered the ultimate shame of having a general break down in combat and abdicate. Col Cochran and Gen Wingate had accomplished their task; they had helped bring the Japanese war machine to its knees. The British 4th Corps still had much fighting to do, but the successful execution of Operation THURSDAY had caused the pendulum to swing in favor of the Allies.

Chapter Six

EPILOGUE

Even before the beginning of the monsoon season of 1944 and the crushing defeat of the Nippon Army at Imphal and Kohima, Gen Arnold recognized the impact of his vision on the Japanese. Shortly after Operation THURSDAY, he began planning the creation of more air commando units. In the 1st Air Commando Group, Gen Arnold had a way of projecting air power without dependence on ground transportation. Applied fully in an area such as Burma, additional air commando units could spare ground forces long, tedious marches where surface lines of communication were sometimes impossible. He planned to deploy four more air commando groups and associated cargo support to India to airlift the British Army further into Central and Southern Burma. Gen Arnold intended to retake that Southeast Asian country from the air! (63:Personal Letter dated 9 July 1986)

As he formulated his strategy, Gen Arnold saw the 1st Air Commando group and the Troop Carrier Command as two pieces of the same puzzle. Lt Gen Barney M. Giles, Deputy Commander of the Army Air Forces, described the inter-relationship of the two types of organizations as follows:

(1) Air Commando Groups are used to initially seize and defend landing sites and later to provide close air support to ground troops.
(2) Combat Cargo Groups are to provide large-scale air transport of ground troops and their supplies to forward areas established by the Air Commando Groups (41:Letter from Lt Gen Barney M. Giles to Lt Gen George C. Kenney, dated 18 June 1944).

Gen Arnold felt the two separate but related organizations were needed to place troops behind enemy lines and keep them supplied, so he proposed to use them in combination. As each Air Commando Group was activated, a Combat Cargo Group would mushroom along side.

By the time Col Alison had returned to the US in April 1944, Gen Arnold had activated two each Air Commando and Combat Cargo Groups. Col Alison was to direct the training of the air commando units and monitor the activation, organization and training of two more groups sometime in the future (63:Personal Letter dated 9 July 1986). Gen Arnold modeled the newly formed 2nd and 3rd Air Commando Groups after the Cochran-Alison original. Each activated air commando unit consisted of the following:

(1) Two P-51 Squadrons of 25 aircraft each with long-range equipment and suitable armament for ground neutralization of the enemy air force;

(2) One Troop Carrier Squadron, highly trained and specialized in gliders—the squadron was equipped with 16 C-47's and 32 CG-4A gliders;

(3) Three Liaison Squadrons, each with 32 litter-carrying L-5's and a small complement of UC-64's; and

(4) Support organizations—one company of airborne engineers, a service group for each two Air Commando Groups, four airdrome squadrons, and one Air Depot Group common to both Air Commando Groups and Combat Cargo Groups.

Once ground soldiers were deployed in the field, Gen Arnold would use the Combat Cargo Group to keep the logistic lifeline open. Each cargo unit was made up of two elements:

(1) Airlift forces consisting of four C-47 Squadrons of 25 aircraft each: Although equipped for double tow, their main job was to move in troops and re-supply them once they began operating in enemy territory, and

(2) Various service organizations: There would be a special

service group for each three Combat Cargo Groups, four airdrome squadrons, and an Aerial Re-supply Depot for packing supplies to be delivered by air (41:Letter from Lt Gen Barney M. Giles to Lt Gen George C. Kenney, dated 18 June 1944).

If all four Air Commando and Combat Cargo organizations had been activated, Gen Arnold's commitment to the reconquest of Burma would have been staggering. In excess of the air assets already in the CBI, Gen Arnold intended to allocate an additional 200 P-51 Mustangs, 464 C-47 Dakotas, 128 CG-4A Waco gliders, 384 L-5 Sentinels, and approximately 50 UC-64 Norsemen! As the planning progressed, the makeup of the Combat Cargo Group was changed to C-46 Commandos, but Gen Arnold's plan was never fully enacted.

After Gen Arnold related his intentions, Col Alison stated that he believed the British would not invade Central and Southern Burma. Alison later explained why by writing, "In this campaign the only two activist officers arguing for the recapture of Burma were General Wingate and General Stilwell who was fighting to reestablish the Burma Road. The British General Staff apparently had other plans, and with the death of General Wingate . . . the momentum for retaking Burma died with him." (63:Personal Letter dated 9 July 1986)

Gen Arnold immediately recalled Col Cochran from the field for confirmation and subsequently visited Sir John Dill, the senior British officer stationed in Washington. Col Alison's evaluation of British intentions was affirmed. Although Gen Arnold fought to keep his idea alive by appealing to Adm Mountbatten, he was rebuffed. The SEAC staff procrastinated and finally agreed to take only one of the units. Gen Arnold tried offering both the 2nd and 3rd Air Commando Groups to Gen Stilwell, but the Infantry General effectively declined when he replied:

To take full advantage . . . I must have troops as competent and as well organized to do the job as your specially trained and organized [Air] Commandos and Combat Cargo units. . . . If you will secure for me one or more American Divisions, I will prove the value of Air Commando units and I think I can make Buck Rogers ashamed of himself (41:Letter from Gen J. W. Stilwell to Gen H. H. Arnold, dated 26 June 1944).

Lacking the support of ground troops to carry out his Southeast Asia strategy, Gen Arnold was forced to discard his dream. Col Alison later explained:

> The 2nd Air Commando Group and the 3rd Air Commando Group were activated and trained in Florida. Activation of the 4th and 5th Groups was cancelled. The 2nd Group along with a Combat Cargo Group [using C-46 Commandos instead of Dakotas] was deployed to India to support operations of the [1st Air Commandos] .... [The] 3rd Group with its associated Combat Cargo Group was deployed to New Guinea for the assault on Mindanao which was the island originally chosen for the landings in the Philippines. Plans changed; Mindanao was bypassed, and the first landings were made on Leyte. There being no special operations required after the landings, the 3rd [Air] Commando Group and its airlift were integrated into the 5th Air Force as operating units. (63:Personal Letter dated 9 July 1986)

Sadly, all three air commando groups shared the same fate. As the fortunes of the war in the Pacific turned to the side of the Allies, conventional units eagerly absorbed the commandos. This action was predictable. As early as 24 March 1944, Air Marshall Baldwin, Commander of the 3rd Tactical Air Force, wrote Gen Stratemeyer, saying, "I do hope that you will be able to arrange to absorb [the 1st Air Commando Group] into the appropriate commands which already exist. The longer this remains an independent outfit working with the Special Force, the harder it is going to be to get it away from Wingate." (41:Letter from Air Marshall John Baldwin to MGen George Stratemeyer, dated 24 March 1944)

Why Gen Arnold's revolutionary airpower strategy did not flourish after the success of the 1st Air Commando Group may best be summed up by B. H. Liddell Hart when he wrote. "The only thing harder than getting a new idea into the military mind is to get an old one out." (9:190) And so the circle closed. The units' autonomy and unorthodoxy—the very elements from which they spawned—were eventually used as arguments to construct a coffin for the air commando idea.

Chapter Seven

CONCLUSIONS

Before closing this study of Gen Arnold's unique strategy, modern military historians need to be aware of more than the evolution and accomplishments of the 1st Air Commando Group. Together, Gen Arnold and the team of Col Cochran and Col Alison inaugurated a heretical concept in airpower employment. First, Gen Arnold imposed conditions on the mission and structural relationship of the 1st Air Commando Group. Then, Col Cochran and Col Alison enhanced the process by constructing a composite air force which was self-sufficient and cut across existing organizational lines. The effect of this combination was more than expected. By examining the 1st Air Commandos, the resulting dynamics of these maverick ideas impacted Operation THURSDAY and the campaign that followed. Simply stated, this combination produced an autonomy which overcame the organizational malaise which existed in SEAC. Gen Arnold's strategy was a success because it addressed the principles of linkage, reality, and future.

Linkage is that element of strategy that assumes objectives are clearly defined, attainable, and acceptable. As the strategy process develops, linkage is the thread that ties ends to means (7:15–16). To understand how Gen Arnold incorporated linkage in the 1st Air Commando Group, a recap of the circumstances in the CBI is required.

The situation in Burma was a classic case of a defensive stalemate—trench warfare without the trenches. Adm Mountbatten's staff prepared numerous plans for the reconquest of Burma, but they scrapped each one. The planners seemed to be stymied by the constraints of materiel and men. In part, the SEAC staff had lost its perspective of the war; in truth, the opening of the Burma Road was inconsistent with British national objectives. Prime Minister Churchill sought a return of the British Empire and, consequently, a weak China. His ability to achieve this desire was exacerbated by Great Britan's overextended economic and industrial conditions. In seeking assistance from the US, Churchill was forced to trade national objectives for war materiel. SEAC's planning staff manifested the resulting lack of linkage by cranking out numerous plans which answered British desires but conflicted with US interests.

Gen Arnold recognized the actions of SEAC and acted to link the 1st Air Commando Group directly with US strategic goals. The US sought to keep the Imperial Japanese troops occupied in China; therefore, the Burma Road was crucial to US and Allied interests in the Pacific. For this reason, Gen Arnold tied Adm Mountbatten's hands by limiting the circumstances for the 1st Air Commando Group's participation in the CBI. Adm Mountbatten was hamstrung by the arrangement. If he wanted more US help, which Britain needed desperately, he would have to follow the dictates of Arnold's conditions. This meant Operation THURSDAY would have to be launched regardless of British desires. As Gen Wingate's plan was the only operation which promised to reopen the land supply artery to China, Gen Arnold took measures to insure his investment. Linkage was achieved; the 1st Air Commando Group acted as the catalyst for actions in the CBI which met US national objectives.

As Col Cochran's men swung into action, the attribute of reality became evident. Reality is the principle that separates facts from illusion (7:17). Gen Arnold knew initiation of Operation THURSDAY was not enough. For the campaign in Northern Burma to succeed, the Chindits would have to be fully and rapidly supported. During the previous Chindit campaign, Gen Wingate had noted deficiencies in the RAF response to his requirements; their procedures were agonizingly slow. In the situation facing the 3rd Indian Division, these inherent delays were totally unacceptable—men's lives were at stake. Gen Arnold faced the reality that adding airplanes and men to the existing SEAC structure would not achieve the desired results. Therefore, Gen Arnold dictated that operational control of the 1st Air Commando Group would reside with Adm Mountbatten. This isolated Col Cochran and his men, thus enabling them to concentrate only on the mission. Totally dedicated to supporting the Chindits, Col Cochran and Col Alison streamlined procedures to achieve responsiveness. Unfettered by competing priorities, the 1st Air Commandos were a service organization in the truest sense of the word.

Finally, Gen Arnold provided for the future by sanctioning the concept of a composite organization. Future is that principle that answers problems by focusing on tomorrow as well as today (7:16). Gen Arnold's first step involved the selection of commanders; Col Cochran and Col Alison meshed to form a dynamic team. The outstanding result of their forward thinking was Operation THURSDAY, the first Allied air invasion in military history. But future was addressed throughout the spectrum of tactics. They encouraged the use of new equipment and concepts. Helicopters, rockets, mobile hospitals, and light planes are examples of their look toward modern weapons. Col Cochran and Col Alison introduced or enlarged the ideas of forward air controllers, airland resupply in tactical operations, and close air support. By crossing vertical lines of orthodox organizational structure, the unit filled the gaps between all elements of airpower—fighters, bombers, transports, and air evacuation. Col Cochran's men established a benchmark in collaboration and cooperation; each member of the air commandos contributed to the accomplishment of the mission. Gen Arnold envisioned the 1st Air Commando Group as an experiment looking toward future air warfare; he achieved his goal.

Gen Arnold broke through the inertia in Burma, created a mission-dedicated organization, and achieved synergy by the skillful use of a maverick strategy. In the book *In Search of Excellence,* the authors speak to the 1st Air Commando Group when they stress the attributes of a bias for action, a focus on the customer, and autonomy and entrepreneurship (17:119–234). The 1st Air Commando Group was the embodiment of those ideals that are recognized today as cornerstones of healthy, progressive institutions. The story of Gen Arnold, Col Cochran, Col Alison, and the men of the 1st Air Commando Group trumpets the might of airpower and the wisdom of a strategy that combines the principles of linkage, reality, and future. By using an unorthodox strategy in aerial warfare, the group serves as a model organization for use in unconventional conflicts.

APPENDIX A

1ST AIR COMMANDO GROUP

Some discrepancies in spelling may exist, but attempt was made to copy as per the original roster of assigned personnel prepared by Headquarters Group as of 12 April 1944.

KEY

* Assigned subsequent to departure of unit from US

D Deceased

M Missing

T Transferred

TSgt	Glen Abell	Cpl	Arthur M. Bowman	Sgt	Carl L. Corbin
TSgt	Carl E. Abernathy	1Lt	Frank M. Bowman*	TSgt	Thomas T. Crabtree
SSgt	Paul H. Abernathy	1Lt	Robert W. Boyd^T	SSgt	John B. Craighead
TSgt	Muncy E. Adams	Sgt	Wayne E. Bozarth	MSgt	Edward Cunningham
SSgt	Lester C. Albrecht	FO	Anthony J. Bracaliello	TSgt	Joe L. Cunningham
FO	Fred W. Alcott	SSgt	Ewald Brenner	Cpl	Jack Curtis
TSgt	Kenneth J. Alexander	Pvt	Thomas A. Briston, Jr.	TSgt	John Damganac
Col	John R. Alison	SSgt	Daniel W. Bunch	TSgt	Sol K. Dansky
SSgt	Alfred T. Almen	TSgt	James Burkhart	1Lt	Elbert E. Davis*
FO	Samuel L. Altman	1Lt	William B. Burns	1Lt	Frank N. Davis*
SSgt	Samuel R. Amspoker	SSgt	Arthur E. Burrell	SSgt	Lemuel A. Davis
1Lt	Gerald L. Arkfield	SSgt	William E. Bussells, Jr.	Capt	William H. S. Davis
Capt	William W. Arnold	Cpl	Claude H. Butler	TSgt	John L. Dean
Cpl	Willie J. Arnold	SSgt	William J. Callison	Capt	John M. DeHoney
WO	Donald M. Armstrong	PFC	Charles J. Campbell	1Lt	Hubert J. Delaney
SSgt	Richard H. Armstrong	PFC	Salvatore Canale	MSgt	Ben J. Delaware, Jr.
Capt	Orlo L. Austin	1Lt	Boyd M. Cannon	Sgt	Robert D. DeMarko
MSgt	Charles N. Baisden	1Lt	Calvert W. Cannon	SSgt	Thomas H. Denlea
FO	Hadley D. Baldwin	SSgt	Leo J. Carroll	1Lt	Charles N. Dennison*
Sgt	Leroy H. Baker	SSgt	Roy C. Carson	PFC	John V. De Palma
Capt	Thomas R. Baker	Capt	Olin B. Carter	TSgt	John C. Derdak
Cpl	William W. Baker	TSgt	William C. Casebolt	1Lt	Murrell J. Dillard^D
Sgt	William C. Barber	SSgt	Benjamin C. Casey	SSgt	Richard M. Dixon
SSgt	Joseph E. Bardzinas	1Lt	Patrick H. Casey	TSgt	Thomas E. Doherty
Capt	Walter B. Barger	SSgt	George H. Caucienne	SSgt	Bernard P. Dole
Capt	Edgar L. Barham	FO	Benjamin C. Cavender*	MSgt	Robert J. Donahue
Sgt	Ralph E. Barker	PFC	Allan E. Center	PFC	Edward J. Donovan
FO	Morris W. Barren	SSgt	Jerry Chalupa, Jr.	1Lt	Robert L. Dowe^D
FO	James S. Bartlett	FO	Robert E. Chambers	1Lt	Patrick J. Driscoll
SSgt	Theodore R. Batchelor	FO	Robert S. Chambers	TSgt	Ralph E. Duddeck
Sgt	George U. Baylies	Sgt	John T. Chasse	Cpl	Jack K. Dunifon
1Lt	Robert E. Beaman^T	SSgt	Woodrow M. Cheek	Sgt	Charles D. Durden
Cpl	Walter L. Beares	SSgt	Arthur M. Cherry	SSgt	Joseph A. D'Urso
1Lt	David C. Beasley*	Maj	William T. Cherry	SSgt	Joseph P. Eagan
Cpl	Robert H. Beatson	SSgt	Jack W. Chesrown	PFC	Robert J. Eason
SSgt	William R. Beaty	MSgt	Robert P. Chew	TSgt	William E. Eckler
SSgt	Charles F. Becker	SSgt	Julian Chiml	Capt	Nelson E. Eddy, Jr.
Cpl	James F. Bedell	PFC	Carlous L. Christian	TSgt	James D. Edenbo
TSgt	James H. Beebe	SSgt	Edward M. Christianson	Capt	Wilbur H. Edwards
Sgt	George W. Beers			Cpl	Wade W. Egelson
Cpl	Thomas R. Behan	SSgt	Eugene L. Chrystler	Maj	Charles L. Englhardt
TSgt	Richard M. Belcher	MSgt	Howard Class	Capt	Cortez F. Enloe, Jr.
MSgt	William J. Bendig	SSgt	Daniel G. Claus	1Lt	Donald I. Erikson
Sgt	Anthony W. Benevit	SSgt	Marion L. Clay	Cpl	James F. Eubank
Capt	Richard L. Benjamin	FO	James T. Clements	SSgt	Rupert S. Eudy
MSgt	Irving Berkowitz	SSgt	Robert L. Clements	CWO	Bruce H. Evans
1Lt	Neal J. Blush	MSgt	Charles J. Ciephas	FO	Robert E. Everett
Maj	Richard W. Boebel	SSgt	Frank M. Clifford	F/Sgt	James C. Ferry
Capt	Neill A. Bollum	Cpl	Joseph L. Cochran	Cpl	John L. Fey
Maj	Ernest O. Bonham	Col	Phillip G. Cochran	Sgt	Charles E. Fisher
1Lt	Ralph C. Bordley	Capt	Edwin J. Coe	SSgt	Robert J. Fiske
1Lt	Frank H. Borowski*D	Capt	Richard E. Cole	Sgt	John D. Fitzgerald
Cpl	Robert S. Bovey	SSgt	Hugh A. Coll	Capt	Paul G. Forcey
F/Sgt	Charles E. Bowden	FO	John L. Coogan	Capt	Irving W. Forde

Capt	John W. Fox	Capt	William B. Hendrick[T]	1Lt	Jack U. Klarr
SSgt	Oswald C. Francisco	FO	Ronald A. Hennig	Sgt	Olin A. Knowles
Cpl	Marion Leo Friday, Jr.	1Lt	Jesse B. Hepler	SSgt	John Koniar, Jr.
SSgt	Duane K. Fudge	SSgt	Doyle H. Herod	SSgt	Nicholas Kosko
Sgt	Walter D. Fulton	1Lt	Carl Hertzer, Jr.[M]	SSgt	John P. Kropp
1Lt	John P. Gabel	SSgt	James W. Hickey*[D]	Capt	Hubert L. Krug[T]
Cpl	Henry A. Galbraith	FO	Thomas A. Hight, Jr.	Cpl	Jack M. Kubler
SSgt	John C. Gallagher	MSgt	Donald L. Hilliard	1Lt	Richard B. Kuenstler[T]
SSgt	Joseph F. Gambill	SSgt	William E. Hitt	Sgt	Peter J. Kuleza
TSgt	Denis T. Garrett	SSgt	Edward F. Hladovcak	PFC	Floyd B. Kyea
SSgt	Loyd W. A. Garrett	1Lt	Brian H. Hodges[D]	Pvt	Claude Lacy
Sgt	John F. Garrity	MSgt	John J. Hoffman	1Lt	Donald A. LaFevre
TSgt	Perry L. Garten	TSgt	Wayne Hoffman	TSgt	Edward LaFortune
Lt Col	Clinton B. Gaty	1Lt	Lloyd D. Hollibough[D]	1Lt	Ralph K. Lanning*
SSgt	Ray C. Geiger	Capt	Neil I. Holm	FO	Erwin H. Lavarre
MSgt	Lawrence R. George	FO	Charles R. Hon	MSgt	Charles M. Lee
FO	Kenneth Georgeson	MSgt	Milo B. Hopper	1Lt	William C. Lehecka
SSgt	Leslie F. Ghastin	SSgt	Ralph E. Horton	Cpl	Martin Levitz
SSgt	Lawrence A. Giargiari	Cpl	Charles I. Hovermale	1Lt	John E. Lewis
TSgt	Thomas H. Gibbons	SSgt	Austin E. Howe	Capt	John K. Lewis, Jr.
Capt	William R. Gilhausen	SSgt	Anton Hrna	Cpl	Loren F. Lewis
Sgt	Earl F. Gillette, Jr.	MSgt	Paul R. Hughes	FO	David H. Lieberman*
SSgt	William Gilliam, Jr.	TSgt	Edward M. Hurly, Jr.	SSgt	Alfred J. Lieto
TSgt	John R. Gilmer	1Lt	Frank M. Huxley	Sgt	Jack A. Lind
1Lt	Richard T. Gilmore	SSgt	John J. Hyland	SSgt	Clarence A. Lingle, Jr.
MSgt	William D. Gleaves, Jr.	Capt	Craig L. Jackson	1Lt	Charles B. Liston[M]
1Lt	Julius Goodman*	SSgt	Austin L. Jameson	SSgt	Robert P. Little
FO	John E. Gotham	Sgt	Ellwood H. Jamison, Jr.	Sgt	Robert A. Livermore
Capt	Don K. Greelis	MSgt	Charles E. Jasper	SSgt	Felix C. Lockman, Jr.
MSgt	George Green	Capt	John H. Jennette	FO	Edmond Lopez
TSgt	Robert R. Greenlund	SSgt	Lynn E. Jennings	TSgt	Joseph C. Lucke
SSgt	George C. Greeson	Cpl	Donald L. Johnson	Sgt	Carl T. Luffman
Capt	Lyle R. Grey*	FO	Howard E. Johnson[M]	1Lt	Robert J. Lundin*
Sgt	John H. Gross	TSgt	John H. Johnson	Capt	Roland R. Lynn
MSgt	Otto C. Gruno	FO	Kenneth Johnson	PFC	James A. Lyon
Sgt	Robert P. Grutsch	Sgt	Ward V. Johnson	TSgt	Joseph Lysowski
SSgt	John C. Gubellini	1Lt	William W. Johnson, Jr.	Sgt	Warren C. MacArtney
1Lt	Frank W. Gursansky*	FO	Burton B. Jones*	Sgt	William J. MacMahon
1Lt	Patrick H. Hadsell	SSgt	Willie P. Jones	TSgt	Finten F. Maegerle
FO	Allen Hall, Jr.	TSgt	Eimer L. Jumper	Cpl	Linn E. Magoffin
SSgt	Matthew B. Hall	TSgt	Francis M. Kaman	Lt Col	Grant Mahoney
FO	Nimrod C. Hall[M]	Sgt	Joseph Kaplan	SSgt	Christopher J. Marion, Jr.
FO	Nimrod F. Hankins	TSgt	Edward L. Karns		
1Lt	Carter Harman	Sgt	Gene O. Kaschel	Sgt	Francis H. Marshall
SSgt	Ben T. Harris, Jr.	Sgt	William R. Keers	TSgt	Dan P. Martin
Cpl	Glenn R. Harsdorff	Capt	Holly M. Keller	FO	Nesbit L. Martin
MSgt	Melvin Haug	FO	Gene A. Kelly	TSgt	Paul W. Mason
MSgt	Thomas J. Hawes	Capt	John A. Kelting[M]	SSgt	Charles E. Maxwell
MSgt	Orval P. Hawkins	SSgt	Miles E. Kempf	F/Sgt	Samuel L. May
Sgt	Edmund F. Haycock	SSgt	Robert J. Kendrigan	SSgt	Clifton F. McCabe
FO	William M. Healy	Cpl	John L. Keranda	Cpl	Joseph P. McCartney
Sgt	Richard Heffman	SSgt	Irwin J. Kersey	TSgt	Lloyd F. McClain
Sgt	Arthur S. Helms	Capt	Marlin F. Kerstetter	SSgt	Bruce H. McCormick
Sgt	Robert E. Henderson	Sgt	John A. Kinner	Cpl	Edgar W. McDowell

Cpl	James F. McDowell	1Lt	Wesley D. Nielson*	TSgt	Texas J. Rankin
TSgt	Elbridge B. McDuff	Cpl	Estil I. NienaberD	TSgt	Fred J. Rannelli
TFO	Bernard P. McGaulley	FO	Vernon Noland	MSgt	Harry A. Raymond
TSgt	Alexander McGregor	SSgt	Bernard Nowakowski	Sgt	John J. Raynak
SSgt	Vernon A. McIninch*D	1Lt	Harold J. Nycum	Maj	Andrew P. ReboriT
FO	Harry L. McKaig	PFC	Carlton H. Ober	Sgt	William G. Reed
1Lt	Archie L. McKay	1Lt	Martin L. O'Berry, Jr.M	TSgt	Louis Reese
Sgt	Thomas C. McLaurin	Sgt	James L. O'Dea	TSgt	Percy W. Reeves
PFC	Harry D. McLean	SSgt	James E. Oliveto	SSgt	Woodrow W. Reynolds
SSgt	Morris B. McManama	MSgt	Arthur R. Olson	Cpl	Silas H. Rhodes
TSgt	Robert F. McMillan	Lt Col	Arvid E. Olson	PFC	John W. Rice
Capt	Leon R. McMullen*	1Lt	Randolph K. Owen	1Lt	James E. Richmond
Cpl	Thomas J. McNally	Sgt	Everette L. Page	Capt	Peter A. Rierson
SSgt	John D. McNamee	Maj	Robert C. Page	Cpl	William B. Ringwood
FO	Martin J. McTigueM	TSgt	Leon S. Palmatier	PFC	William A. Rintz
SSgt	John Meck	1Lt	Fred P. Paris	SSgt	Clarence F. Ripple
TSgt	Sam Meiner	FO	Bishop ParrottD	FO	William C. RitzingerD
1Lt	Robley B. Melton	SSgt	Russell L. Parrott, Jr.	PFC	Maurice R. Roberts
SSgt	Harold C. Mendelson	FO	Jim Patterson	PFC	Robert L. Roberts
Sgt	William C. Mercer	SSgt	Robert J. Patterson	SSgt	Stamford N. Robertson
1Lt	Frank B. Merchant	TSgt	Winston G. Pearson	FO	James K. RollinsT
1Lt	John E. Meyer	TSgt	Arnold Pederson	Capt	Vincent J. Rose
1Lt	Carwin A. Miles	FO	Clifford C. Pederson	SSgt	Floyd J. Rosenhahn
Capt	Donald V. MillerM	1Lt	Stanley Pelcak*	SSgt	Willard L. Roy
Cpl	Donald W. Miller	SSgt	Eric Peterson	PFC	Alfred I. Royce
Sgt	Ernest O. Miller, Jr.	Maj	Robert L. Petit	SSgt	Robert N. Ruehien
Cpl	George R. Miller	Sgt	Chester Petrowsky	FO	Eugene L. Ruiz
PFC	John J. Miller	SSgt	Rodney E. Petty, Jr.	SSgt	Raymond J. Ruksas
Sgt	Leonard J. Miller	MSgt	Kendal J. Pfeilsticker	MSgt	Ray R. Rumfelt
SSgt	Clyde Millstead	Sgt	James D. Phelan	Cpl	Forest J. Russell
1Lt	Daniel B. Mitchell*	Capt	Duke Phillips, Jr.	1Lt	Charles L. Russhon
MSgt	John A. Mitchell	Sgt	Albert E. Piester	F/Sgt	James J. Ryan
Capt	Mack A. Mitchell	TSgt	John C. Pink	TSgt	Frank Sadoski*D
FO	Billy Mohr	1Lt	Younger A. Pitts, Jr.	SSgt	Walter J. Sakowski
Capt	Robert E. Moist	1Lt	Alvin J. Plouff	SSgt	Lloyd I. Samp
1Lt	Charles F. Moore	SSgt	Alexander Podlecki	Capt	John C. Sanichez
SSgt	James W. Moore	Sgt	Lawrence N. Poepping	Maj	Jacob P. Sartz
Capt	Temple C. Moore	TSgt	Walter J. Polak	Cpl	Joe P. Satarino
PFC	Marvin C. Morgan	Sgt	Cyrus C. Porter	FO	Maryln O. Satrom
PFC	William H. Morison	MSgt	John H. Porter	Sgt	William J. Schatz
PFC	Harold E. Mueller	1Lt	Andrew B. Postlewait	PFC	Robert J. Schieierstein
SSgt	Bernard V. Mulvahill, Jr.	1Lt	Curt C. PowellD	TSgt	Karl K. Schmidt
		Cpl	Kenneth J. Powell	TSgt	Edward W. Schnatzmeyer
TSgt	Irvin L. Murphy	TSgt	Russell E. Prather		
Sgt	James B. Murphy	Sgt	Michael P. Presti	Capt	Erle H. SchneiderM
Capt	Weldon O. Murphy	SSgt	William H. Pretz	1Lt	Soloman Schnitzer
Capt	Lester K. MurrayT	FO	John H. Price, Jr.	1Lt	Ned Schramm, Jr.
Sgt	Thomas F. Murray	Sgt	Thomas E. Purcell	SSgt	Harry J. Schroderer
PFC	Howard G. Myers, Jr.	SSgt	Grant P. Putnam	SSgt	Marshall G. Schuier
Sgt	William H. NeffD	SSgt	Lewis J. Qualkenbush	SSgt	Hal H. Schurler
1Lt	Louis R. Newell	Cpl	Jennings B. Rader	SSgt	Robert C. Schurr
FO	John F. Newland	Maj	Walter V. Radovitch	FO	John L. Sciez*
SSgt	John A. Nicholson	FO	Francis L. Randall	1Lt	Virgil E. Scoobey
1Lt	Fay L. Nielsen*D	Sgt	George F. Randall	FO	Edward G. Scott

110

PFC	John W. Seagran	TSgt	Harley V. Sutton	1Lt	Stephen A. Wanderer*D
1Lt	Donald E. Seese	PFC	Joseph S. Sweeney	1Lt	Albert T. Ward
SSgt	Peter C. Serio	SSgt	Walter R. Sweeney	TSgt	Owen C. Warren
1Lt	Joe Setnor*	SSgt	Shyojiro T. Taketa	SSgt	John Watson
Sgt	Don K. Settles	Cpl	Charles A. Tanner	Sgt	Roy Watson
1Lt	James E. Sever	FO	James W. Tate	Cpl	Warren G. Watts
1Lt	Robert P. SharrockD	1Lt	Emery D. Taylor	SSgt	Walter R. Waugh, Jr.
FO	Troy C. Shaw	Maj	William H. Taylor, Jr.	FO	Mainord M. Weaver
FO	LeRoy C. ShimulunasM	SSgt	Fred S. Teal	Cpl	Max V. Weaver
1Lt	Jackson J. Shinkle	TSgt	Andrew M. Ternosky	TSgt	Jack H. Webb
Cpl	Charles E. Siason	WO	John M. Teten	1Lt	Wesley D. Weber*
Capt	Daniel A. Sinskie	PFC	Donald E. Thomas	SSgt	Jesse C. Webster
FO	Dean D. Skelton*	1Lt	Robert D. ThomasD	Cpl	Robert J. Weeks
Capt	Everett F. SmithT	SSgt	Jasper C. Thompson	SSgt	Selig Weinstein
Sgt	Frank H. Smith	Sgt	Ngon T. TomD	PFC	Morris Weiss
MSgt	George Smith	MSgt	Kermit G. Torkelson	1Lt	Kenneth L. WellsD
SSgt	Harlan P. Smith	Cpl	Robert E. True	TSgt	Leslie E. Werner
SSgt	Harold L. Smith	Sgt	Clifford J. Tucker	FO	Russell J. WestT
Capt	Lewis S. Smith	Capt	Donald C. TullochM	TSgt	James R. Westmoreland
Lt Col	Robert T. Smith	SSgt	Alfred E. Turkingham	Maj	Edwin S. White
Maj	Samson Smith	FO	Charles B. Turner	Sgt	Warren G. Wilcox
TSgt	Zane L. Smith	1Lt	Frank M. Turney	1Lt	Malcolm J. Wilkins*
TSgt	Glen W. Snyder	1Lt	Leo S. Tyszecki*	SSgt	Chet A. Willets, Jr.
SSgt	Richard D. Snyder	1Lt	Vincent L. Ulery	FO	Bruce Williams
CWO	Burton E. Sommers	1Lt	Steve T. Uminski	1Lt	Grant H. Wilson, Jr.
1Lt	Milton H. Sparks*	Cpl	Milan J. Urbancic	1Lt	Elmer L. (Jack) Wingo*
SSgt	Joseph H. Sparrow	Sgt	Charles J. Usey	1Lt	Robert A. Wink*
Cpl	John E. Sprague	1Lt	Charles J. Vagim*	Capt	James R. Woods
MSgt	Gordon C. Spurlock	1Lt	Aurele. R. Van De	Cpl	Gerald L. Young
TSgt	Gerald W. Stake	Wehge*		Sgt	Walter E. Young
Sgt	John J. Stalker, Jr.	1Lt	Fred H. Van Wagner*	F/Sgt	Arnold Z. Zahorsky
WO	Peter E. Stefonich	SSgt	Arthur H. Van Wye	Sgt	Stanley G. Zajack
FO	Walter W. Steinke	TSgt	Geoffrey S. Vore	Sgt	Alexander Zalman
FO	Samuel F. Steinmark	TSgt	Norman W. Wach	PFC	Morris H. Zalmonovich
Sgt	Calvin B. Stewart	Capt	Edward (Sam)Wagner	Sgt	Michael R. Zamenski
1Lt	Eimer J. StoneD	FO	Robert Wagner	PFC	Carl J. Zarcone
Sgt	John A. Stroebeck	1Lt	Howell T. Walker	Capt	Carl E. Ziegler, Jr.
SSgt	Franklin O. Suckow	FO	Earl C. Waller	FO	Leo Zuk
PFC	L. D. Sutherland	SSgt	Preston W. Walling		
Sgt	Enoch V. Sutton	SSgt	William T. Walters		

111

BIBLIOGRAPHY

A. REFERENCES CITED

Books

1. Bateson, Charles. *The War With Japan; A Concise History*. Hong Kong: Michigan State University Press. 1968.

2. Bidwell, Shelford. *The Chindit War; Stilwell, Wingate, and the Campaign in Burma: 1944*. New York: Macmillan Publishing Co., Inc. 1979.

3. Burchette, W. C. *Wingate Adventure*. Melbourne: F. W. Cheshire. Pty. Ltd. 1944.

4. Calvert, Michael. *Prisoners of Hope*. London: Jonathan Cape, 1952.

5. Cate, James L. and Wesley F. Cravens (eds.). *The Army Air Forces in World War II, Vol IV*. Chicago: University of Chicago Press, 1948.

6. Christian, John L. *Burma*. London: Wm. Collins & Son & Co., Ltd., 1945.

7. Drew, Dennis M., Lt Col, USAF and Dr. Donald M. Snow. *Introduction to Strategy*. Maxwell AFB, AL: Air University, 1985.

8. Esposito, Col Vincent J. (ed). *The West Point Atlas of American Wars; Volume II, 1900–1953*. New York: Frederick A. Praeger, 1959.

9. Heinl, Robert D., Jr. *Dictionary of Military and Naval Quotations*. Annapolis, Md: United States Naval Institute, 1984.

10. Kirby, S. Woodburn, et al (ed). *The War Against Japan; Volume II India's Most Dangerous Hour*. London: Her Majesty's Stationery Office, 1958.

11. _____. *The War Against Japan; Volume III The Decisive Battles*. London: Her Majesty's Stationery Office, 1961.

12. Masters, John. *The Road Past Mandalay*. New York: Harper & Row, Publishers, Inc., 1961.

13. Matthews, Geoffrey, *The Re-conquest of Burma 1943–1945*. Aldershot, UK: Gale & Polden Limited, 1966.

14. Mende, Tibor. *South-east Asia between Two Worlds*. London: Turnstile Press, 1955.

15. Moraes, F. R. and Stimson, Robert. *Introduction to India*. London: Oxford University Press., 1946.

16. Moser, Don (ed). *China-Burma-India*. Alexandria, Va: Time-Life Books, 1978.

17. Peters, Thomas J. and Robert H. Waterman. *In Search of Excellence*. New York: Harper and Row, Publishers, Inc., 1982.

18. Rolo, Charles J. *Wingate's Raiders*. London: George G. Harrap & Co. Ltd., 1944.

19. Romanus, Charles F. and Sunderland, Riley (ed). *United States Army in World War II: China-Burma-India Theater; Stilwell's Mission to China*. Washington DC: Office of the Chief of Military History, 1953.

20. _____. *United States Army in World War II: China-Burma-India Theater; Stilwell's Command Problems*. Washington DC: Office of the Chief of Military History, 1956.

21. Slim, Field Marshall, the Viscount. *Defeat into Victory*. New York: 1961.

22. Smith, E. D. *Battle for Burma*. New York: Holmes & Meier Publishers, Inc., 1979.

23. Swimson, Arthur. *The Battle of Kohima*. New York: Stein and Day, 1967.

24. Sykes, Christopher. *Orde Wingate; A Biography*. Cleveland: World Publishing Co., 1959.

25. Thomas, Lowell. *Back to Mandalay*. New York: The Greystone Press, 1951.

26. Tuchman, Barbara W. *Stilwell and the American Experience in China, 1911–45*. New York: Macmillan Publishing Co., Inc., 1970.

27. Tulloch, Derek (ed). *Wingate In Peace and War*. London: Macdonald and Co., Ltd, 1972.

Articles and Periodicals

28. Arnold, H. H. "The Aerial Invasion of Burma." *National Geographic Magazine*, Vol. LXXXVI, No. 2 (August 1944), pp. 129–148.

29. Bainbridge, John. " 'Flip Corkin.' " *Life*, Vol. 15, No. 6 (9 August 1943), pp. 42–28.

30. "British Raid Burma." *Life*, (28 June 1943), pp. 19–24.

31. Caulfield, D. C. "The Bright Flame." *Marine Corps Gazette*, Vol. 48, No. 10 (October 1964), pp. 41–46.

32. McCann, John A., Col, USAF. "Air Power and 'The Man'." *Air Power Historian*, Vol. 6, No. 2 (April 1959), pp. 108–124.

33. Prather, Russel E. "Broadway Burma." *Ex-CBI Roundup*, Vol. 22, No. 10, (December 1967), pp. 6–10.

34. _____, "Easy Into Burma, Part I." *Ex-CBI Roundup*, Vol. 21, No. 2, (February 1966), pp. 8–25.

35. _____, "Easy Into Burma, Part II." *Ex CBI Roundup*, Vol. 21, No. 3, (March 1966), pp. 8–25.

36. Sciutti, W. J., Capt, USAF. "The First Air Commando Group August 1943–May 1944." *American Aviation Historical Society Journal*, Vol. 13, No. 2 (Fall 1968), pp. 178–185.

Official Documents

37. AAFSAT, Intelligence. Glider Operations on Two Fronts; Special Intelligence Report No. 54, September 1944. 248.532–63, in USAF Collection, USAFHRC.

38. AC/AS, Intelligence. Air Room interview with Lt Col John R. Alison, 3 July 1943. 142.052, in USAF Collection, USAFHRC.

39. AC/AS, Intelligence. Special Informational Intelligence Report No. 43-11; Interview with Lt Col Philip G. Cochran, 28 June 1943. 142.034-2, in USAF Collection, USAFHRC.

40. AC/AS, Intelligence. Chronological History of Project 9 (Cochran), 17 August 1943–28 January 1944. 142–0411–9, in USAF Collection, USAFHRC.

41. AC/AS, Plans. 1st Air Commando Force and Combat Cargo Groups organization and redeployment correspondence and memoranda, 1943–45. 145.81–170, in USAF Collection, USAFHRC.

42. AC/AS, Plans. Interview with Col John R. Alison, 25 April 1944. 145.95, in USAF Collection, USAFHRC.

43. British Air Ministry. *Operations in Burma, 15 Dec 1941–20 May 1942.* 512.952, in USAF Collection, USAFHRC.

44. British Information Service. *Victory in Burma.* New York: British Government, 1945. 168.7097–13, in Ronald F. Kennedy Collection, USAFHRC.

45. Burma Research Society. *Burma Facts and Figures.* London: Longmans, Green & Co. Ltd., 1946.

46. Central Office of Information. *The Campaign in Burma.* London: His Majesty's Stationery Office, 1946.

47. HQ 3TAF. Photographic report of 1st Air Commando Force, September 1944. 822.08, in USAF Collection, USAFHRC.

48. JICA/CBI. First Air Commando Force Invasion of Burma; Report No. 1448, 29 March 1944. 810.6091A, in USAF Collection, USAFHRC.

49. JICA/CBI. Glider Operations in Burma; Report No. 1449, 1 April 1944. 810.6091A, in USAF Collection, USAFHRC.

50. JICA/CBI. Report of Troop Carrier Command Participation in THURSDAY Operation; Report No. 1579, 16 March 1944. 810.6091A, in USAF Collection, USAFHRC.

51. JICA/CBI. Wingate Report on Airborne Invasion of Burma; Report No. 1833, 12 April 1944. 810.6091A, in USAF Collection USAFHRC.

52. JICA/CBI. Supplemental Report on First Air Commando Force (Group) in Burma; Report No. 1834, 15 April 1944. 810.6091A, in USAF Collection, USAFHRC.

53. JICA/CBI. Final Operations of First Air Commando Group in Burma; Report No. 3137, 30 May 1944. 810.6091A, in USAF Collection, USAFHRC.

54. JICA/CBI. Light Plane Operations of the First Air Commando Group in Burma; Report No. 3138, 5 June 1944. 810.6091A, in USAF Collection, USAFHRC.

55. Office, Chief of Military History. Burma Operation record, 15th Army operations in Imphal area and withdrawal to North Burma, 10 October 1952. K171.41-134, in USAF Collection, USAFHRC.

56. Oral History Interview. Interview of Philip G. Cochran by Dr. James C. Hasdorff, 20 October 1975. K239.0512–876, in USAF Collection, USAFHRC.

57. Oral History Interview. Interview of John R. Alison by Kenneth Leish, July 1960, K146.34–2, in USAF Collection, USAFHRC.

58. SEAC. Supreme Allied Commander's Dispatch covering SEAC Strategy and Operations, August 1943–September 1945. 805.04A, in USAF Collection, USAFHRC.

59. SEAC, Air Command. Collected reports and plans on Operation THURSDAY, March–April 1944. 815.452, in USAF Collection, USAFHRC.

60. Unit History: 1st Air Commando Group. History of 1st Air Commando Group, September 1943–August 1945. GP–A–CMDO–1–HI, USAF Collection, USAFHRC.

61. Unit History: 1st Air Commando Group. History of First Air Commando Group from 1943. K–GP–A–CMDO–1–HI, in USAF Collection, USAFHRC.

Unpublished Materials

62. Moist, Robert E. "Basha Blabber." 1st Air Commando Association Newsletter, August 1979–November/December 1985.

Other Sources

63. Alison, John R. Presentation to ACSC Class of 1985. Maxwell AFB, AL, 36112. Video tape recording, Air University Television Center, Maxwell AFB, Al.

64. Interview with Burma Rifle, Chindit. Orlando, Fl, 12 Oct 85. Notes, personal possession, Maxwell AFB, Al.

65. Interview with 1st Air Commando Bomber (B–25), Light-Cargo (US–64), and Liaison (L–1/L–5) Pilot. Orlando, Fl, 12 Oct 85. Video tape recording and effects, personal possession, Maxwell AFB, Al.

66. Interview with 1st Air Commando Fighter (P–51A) Pilot. Orlando, Fl, 11 Oct 85. Video tape recording, personal possession, Maxwell AFB, Al.

67. Interview with 1st Air Commando Glider (CG–4A) Flight Officer. Orlando, Fl, 10 Oct 85. Notes, personal possession, Maxwell AFB, Al.

68. Interview with 1st Air Commando Liaison (L–1/L–5) Pilots. Orlando, Fl, 12 Oct 85. Video tape recording, personal possession, Maxwell AFB, Al.

69. Interview with 1st Air Commando Transport (C–47) Pilots. Orlando, Fl, 12 Oct 85. Video tape recording, personal possession, Maxwell AFB, Al.

B. RELATED SOURCES

Books

Greenfield, Kent Roberts (ed). *Command Decisions.* Washington DC: Office of the Chief of Military History, 1960.

King, Barbara P., Maj, USAF and Edward M. Leete, Maj, USAF. *The 1st Air Commando Group of World War II: An Historical Perspective.* Maxwell AFB, AL: Air University, 1977.

Mrazek, James E. *The Glider War.* New York: St. Martin's Press, Inc., 1975.

Toland, John. *The Rising Sun.* New York: Random House, Inc., 1970.

Articles and Periodicals

Cunningham, Ed. "Cochran's Commandos." *Yank*, Vol. 1, No. 38 (22 April 1944), pp. 41–46.

Mead, P. W. "The Chindit Operations of 1944." *Royal United Service Institution Journal*, Vol. 100, No. 597 (February 1955), pp. 250–262.

Official Documents

Eastern Air Command. Collected narrative reports of operations in CBI Theater from December 1943–May 1945. 820.306, in USAF Collection, USAFHRC.

SEAC, Troop Carrier Command. Diary of the Commanding General [Gen Old], 15 December 1943–4 June 1944. 833.13–1, in USAF Collection, USAFHRC.

United States Forces, India Burma Theater. Operations Journal of Gen Stilwell's headquarters covering operations of Chinese and British Forces in Burma during the period 16 March 1942–2 May 1942. 810.305–1, in USAF Collection, USAFHRC

ABOUT THE AUTHOR

Major R. D. Van Wagner graduated from Texas Tech University in 1969 with a Bachelor of Business Administration degree in Advertising. He was commissioned from Officer Training School in April 1971 and finished Undergraduate Navigator Training as a Distinguished Graduate of Class 72-13. In his follow-on assignment to C-141 Starlifters at Norton AFB, while still a First Lieutenant, he upgraded to Select Lead Airdrop Navigator and Flight Examiner. At Norton, he completed programs with the USAF Audio Visual Service which led to the award of an AFSC in Television Production. Transferred to Mather AFB in 1975, he worked in the Trainer Systems Division developing software modifications to the T45 Navigator Simulator. In 1979, he completed a Masters degree in Systems Management from the University of Southern California just in time to be sent to the Military Airlift Command Aircrew Training Center at Altus AFB. There in addition to being a flight instructor, he was a classroom instructor, a curriculum developer, the Chief of C-141 Navigator Training, and the CINCMAC navigator on Gen James Allen's crew. In 1982, he was selected for the Air Force Institute of Technology Education with Industry program. After a tour with IBM in the Quality Assurance option, he transferred to Kelly AFB in a career broadening assignment as a contract negotiator. Maj Van Wagner is a Distinguished Graduate of Air Command and Staff College, Class of 1986.